Matt—

Thank you for your commitment to teaching your organization how to hire and retain the best!

Adam

PRAISE FOR *THE BEST TEAM WINS*

"The difference between success and failure for most new ventures is the quality of the team. *The Best Team Wins* is a must-read for high-growth founders and CEOs."

—**Troy Henikoff,** Managing Director, Techstars

"The secret to amazing customer experience is having an amazing team. If you want to learn how to build the best team in your industry, read this book!"

—**John R. DiJulius III,** author of
The Customer Service Revolution

"In *The Best Team Wins* Adam Robinson has created a complete guide to the recruitment and hiring process for business owners and hiring managers. HR pros will also pick up pointers in a volume packed with well-thought-out, and tested, specific recommendations on topics that are usually fraught with generalities including cultural fit, attitude, competencies, and the value of passive candidates. Read the book cover to cover for the complete picture or choose among the many included templates such as the job profile, telephone interview format, reference checks, and offer letter. Either way, you have concepts to put to good use and improve the quality of your hires."

—**Rebecca Mazin,** HR Consultant, Recruit Right,
Coauthor of *The HR Answer Book*

THE BEST
TEAM WINS

ADAM ROBINSON

THE BEST
TEAM WINS

BUILD YOUR BUSINESS
THROUGH PREDICTIVE HIRING

GREENLEAF
BOOK GROUP PRESS

Published by Greenleaf Book Group Press
Austin, Texas
www.gbgpress.com

Distributed by Greenleaf Book Group

For ordering information or special discounts for bulk purchases, please contact Greenleaf Book Group at PO Box 91869, Austin, TX 78709, 512.891.6100.

Design and composition by Greenleaf Book Group
Cover design by Greenleaf Book Group
Cover Images: © Hurst Photo, 2016. Used under license from Shutterstock.com.
©iStockphoto.com/michaeljung

Cataloging-in-Publication data is available.

Print ISBN: 978-1-62634-382-5

eBook ISBN: 978-1-62634-383-2

Part of the Tree Neutral® program, which offsets the number of trees consumed in the production and printing of this book by taking proactive steps, such as planting trees in direct proportion to the number of trees used: www.treeneutral.com

TreeNeutral

Printed in the United States of America on acid-free paper

17 18 19 20 21 22   10 9 8 7 6 5 4 3 2 1

First Edition

CONTENTS

INTRODUCTION

Why are most companies so bad at hiring?

This question has been on my mind for the better part of two decades, starting with my first job as a recruiter in the staffing industry and continuing through my journey as a technology entrepreneur. People are almost always the single largest expense in a company's budget, yet most companies have a better process for buying office supplies than they do for hiring great talent. *Why?*

The answer to this question is amazingly straightforward: *Most companies are bad at hiring because most companies don't teach their managers how to do it.* Think about the last time you received formal training on hiring. I won't hold my breath waiting for an answer, because more than 90 percent of companies lack any kind of structured hiring process. It's no wonder that the average hiring success rate for companies is less than 50 percent.

The good news here is that companies can dramatically improve their hiring results by implementing a structured hiring process and teaching their managers how to follow it. As the cofounder and CEO of Hireology, a talent technology company that I began in 2010, I'm fortunate to have the opportunity to work with thousands of entrepreneurs, CEOs, and managers every year to address the specific hiring challenges that they face. When we launched Hireology, our vision for the company was straightforward and personal: *empower business owners to succeed by helping them build their best possible team.* We'd been there as business owners, and we'd made all of the typical hiring mistakes.

Nobody had ever taught us how to "do it right," and we had the battle scars to prove it. We knew there had to be a better way.

Six years later, we're incredibly humbled that over 5,000 businesses are using Hireology's platform to source, screen, hire, and onboard their teams. Along the way, we've created a process that, when followed, leads to higher quality hires, lower administrative costs, a lower cost-per-hire, and significantly reduced twelve-month turnover. These results aren't attainable only by big corporations—we've remained steadfast in our focus on delivering value to the entrepreneur: the family-owned automotive group; the franchisee; the business services provider; the high-tech start-up; the Main Street retailer—men and women who, like you, risk their personal capital every day to compete in some of the toughest markets.

I've written this book to share with you the processes, tricks, and tools that I've developed over the last twenty years to turn hiring from a liability into a source of sustainable competitive advantage for your business. You don't have to be a Fortune 500 company to succeed in the hiring game. You do, however, need to implement a consistent, repeatable process and measure the right things. But rest assured—*you can do this.*

This book isn't theory; it's a blueprint that will take you step-by-step through the hiring process, from writing the job profile and sourcing candidates all the way through to specific interview questions and testing approaches. Throughout the book, you'll hear from real entrepreneurs and business leaders who have experienced the same struggles that you have:

- You'll meet franchise industry veteran David Barr, whose company, PMTD Restaurants, owns twenty-three restaurants across several states. David credits his company's focus on people (the initials stand for "People Make the Difference," after all) for the success he's achieved.

- You'll hear from Tim Heitmann, founder and CEO of Popcorn Palace, whose company has made the Inc. 5000 list of America's fastest-growing private companies an unprecedented ten years in a row.

- You'll listen to Joe Turchyn, a veteran of the retail automotive industry and director of corporate strategy and development at Burns Buick GMC in New Jersey, share how small but important changes to his dealerships' hiring model has his stores humming.

- You'll learn from technology entrepreneur Ajay Goel, founder and CEO of JangoMail, as he talks about the mistakes he made—and the lessons he learned—as he grew his start-up from bootstrapped concept to a successful acquisition.

- You'll hear from Michael Krasman, founder of several high growth businesses, about the challenges of finding the right fit for your company culture.

- You'll find out how Cathi Trippe, a senior leader at Phil Long Dealerships, rewired the organization's approach to hiring and risk management after the 2008 recession—and how these moves generated game-changing results.

- You'll learn from the perspective of human capital strategist Candice Crane, and learn why employment brand and onboarding is critical for the success of your business.

- You'll understand from serial entrepreneur Jeff Ellman that sometimes the best candidate has *zero* experience in your industry.

- You'll find out from VP of HR at SAVO Tracy McCarthy that paying more for a candidate with more experience doesn't pay equal dividends for your company.

- And you'll learn from nationally renowned restaurant operator, author, and speaker Nick Sarillo how businesses of any size and makeup can find and retain great talent.

Can you imagine the impact that getting your hiring decisions right seven, even eight times out of ten would have on the growth and profitability of your business? My hope is that by reading this book and implementing these ideas, you'll unlock the amazing potential in your business. I'm here to tell you that *you can do this.*

Read on, and turn your company's hiring process into a source of sustainable competitive advantage that will pay dividends for years to come.

STAGE ONE:

DEFINE
THE ROLE

Chapter One

DISCOVER YOUR UNTAPPED COMPETITIVE ADVANTAGE

When you distill business to its basic element, you're left with one thing: people. No matter what product or service you're offering—selling cars, renting hotel rooms, manufacturing 3D printers, or providing digital marketing services—it's the people working in your business that make things happen. They're the faces that your customers see on a daily basis. In today's hypercompetitive world, where your competitors can copy even the most innovative new offerings in near real time, it's your people that are the *true* secret. Good people clear the field and drive success. They are the one truly unique competitive advantage left for your business to pursue.

Even though payroll is one of the largest expenses for a business, most businesses have woefully inadequate processes to ensure that the right people get hired. People account for around 70 percent of the cost structure of a typical company; think of your people as stacks of cash walking around in shoes. When a manager makes a bad hire, an employee can end up costing the company even more—up to ten times a typical employee's compensation, by some estimates. Why is the financial damage of a poor hiring decision so high? Bad hires result in the following costs:

- Disruption to your company culture that negatively influences your other employees

- Loss of essential management time and focus because of turnover and recruiting

- Damage to your company's reputation, which affects your customers and future potential employees

- Wasted wages and training costs

Despite these high stakes, most managers report that nearly 50 percent of the people who report to them fail to meet performance expectations, a problem that often occurs when employees do not understand how their performance is measured.[1] With results like these, why even bother with a hiring process or job interviews? Why not just flip a coin, hire all the heads, and save yourself the trouble? If good people are so crucial to the success of your business, isn't it about time to even those odds by rethinking how you might go about hiring them?

Finding qualified candidates is harder than ever.

"Labor shortages in crucial functional areas such as technology, sales, and marketing are making it all but impossible for companies to meet their talent needs solely with traditional recruiting techniques like job postings—a trend we expect to intensify, given the growth of the worldwide knowledge economy," says Corey Greendale, a technology venture capitalist and analyst with the firm First Analysis.

"The global economic recovery is shifting power from employers

---

1   Jim Harter, "Obsolete Annual Reviews: Gallup's Advice," *Gallup*, September 28, 2015, http://www.gallup.com/opinion/gallup/185921/obsolete-annual-reviews-gallup-advice.aspx.

to employees with high-demand skills and increasingly turning labor into a seller's market."

Greendale also notes that demographics are likely to exacerbate this trend, with the Bureau of Labor Statistics projecting that US workers aged sixteen to twenty-four will shrink 13.3 percent in the decade ending 2022.

FIG 1.1—SIZE OF ENTRY LEVEL US LABOR FORCE
(IN THOUSANDS)

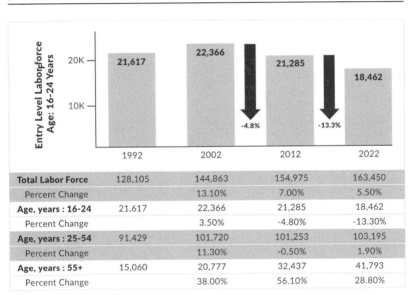

	1992	2002	2012	2022
Total Labor Force	128,105	144,863	154,975	163,450
Percent Change		13.10%	7.00%	5.50%
Age, years : 16-24	21,617	22,366	21,285	18,462
Percent Change		3.50%	-4.80%	-13.30%
Age, years : 25-54	91,429	101,720	101,253	103,195
Percent Change		11.30%	-0.50%	1.90%
Age, years : 55+	15,060	20,777	32,437	41,793
Percent Change		38.00%	56.10%	28.80%

"Business leaders worldwide increasingly recognize that talent will be a key competitive consideration over the coming years," says Greendale. "HR systems and structures are often insufficient to address the looming challenges."

The 2013 Conference Board CEO Challenge report, a survey of seven hundred CEOs from around the globe, identified human capital as the number one challenge facing them today, above factors such as operational excellence (number two) and customer relationships (number four).

"We view these results as a signal that human capital is shifting from a seat filling function to a core strategic consideration and will increasingly occupy the attention of high-level corporate decision makers," says Greendale.

Getting the right people in your organization isn't someone else's job anymore: It's time for you to *own it.*

Case Study: People Make the Difference

David Barr has seen it all when it comes to running retail and restaurant businesses. He has advice for business owners and hiring managers: It's time to rethink your hiring practices. The factor that sets any business apart from its competitors is its people.

"Hiring the right people is the number one thing we do in retail," says Barr, whose holding company is called PMTD (People Make the Difference). "Our people are the most crucial factor to our success. It doesn't matter whether we sell burgers, chicken, or jewelry. We will win every time if we have the best people. They are the representation of our brand and the interface with our customers."

Given his extensive experience as a business owner and advisor, Barr has been asked to brief White House policymakers, senators, and members of Congress and their staffs on how different policies like the Affordable Care Act (ACA) influence the retail industry. The retail industry employs more than fifteen million people in the US,[2] which

2   United States Department of Labor, "Industry employment and output projections to 2024," Bureau of Labor Statistics, 2015, http://www.bls.gov/opub/mlr/2015/article/industry-employment-and-output-projections-to-2024-1.htm.

means about one in ten people in the workforce are employed in the retail sector—more than any other market segment except government and healthcare.

The retail industry is a bellwether for the rest of the economy. This important status means the forces buffeting the labor market, such as the crunch caused by retiring Baby Boomers and pressure to raise the minimum wage, are hitting retail businesses particularly hard. It's becoming harder and harder to find good people. It's going to get even harder in coming years.

Barr has done a great deal of hiring over his career, from frontline workers all the way up to the C-suite level. Although the process of interviewing and hiring an hourly employee may be different than bringing on a new CEO, Barr believes that everyone, regardless of their position, wakes up with the same needs and desires.

"Everyone wants to work for something that is bigger than themselves," says Barr. "They don't want to just punch a clock. You have to find people who don't just want a job—they want an opportunity."

When Barr evaluates candidates at any level of his organization, he first looks to see if the candidate has the kind of intelligence and attitude that fits their culture. The applicants' technical ability and their match with the job description come second.

"We want to hire for attitude and train for aptitude in the retail business," he says.

Barr prioritizes candidates who display basic attributes like an ability to make good eye contact and be polite. To illustrate his preferences, Barr shares a legend about Debbie Fields, the eponymous founder of Mrs. Fields Cookies. Fields would interview candidates in a public space, such as the middle of a mall food court. She would ask her candidates to stand up and belt out a hearty rendition of "Happy Birthday."

"If someone wasn't willing to be courageous and bold enough to do something self-deprecating like that, they wouldn't be a fit at a retail counter," says Barr.

For frontline workers, Barr says it's essential to cast a wide net when you're building your applicant pool. This large scope increases your chances at identifying qualified candidates who fit your culture. For executives, Barr says he relies on a more targeted approach where he uses internal referrals or networking sites like LinkedIn to tap potential new hires.

Before you go looking to hire someone, it's important that you first understand exactly what you are hiring that person to do.

"You don't want to fall in love with someone and then stretch the position beyond what they are capable of," says Barr.

When managers focus too much on just filling out their open position, they can make bad hires. A bad hire costs an organization enormous amounts of money and time. Worse, a bad hire can also become a cancer inside your organization.

"If you hire a bad manager who treats people poorly and doesn't make them believe they are achieving great things as a team," says Barr, "then you won't attract great people. You will see the results of that in your business."

Barr says that developing a scalable hiring process that prioritizes identifying the people who are the best fit for your organization is the biggest factor in whether your business will be successful or not.

Taking Control of the Hiring Process

Hiring is the last crucial component of your business where you have total control. Think about it: We live in an era where your business faces increasing pressure and risk, from competition to regulation. You control fewer and fewer of the variables that determine your business's success. You can't control interest rates, access to capital markets, constantly shifting consumer behavior, or rapid industry consolidation. You also can't control the decisions made by the Consumer Financial Protection Bureau, or the fact that Congress passes game-changing laws like the Affordable Care Act. The only thing you have *100 percent* control over is the employees you put on your payroll. It's time to give hiring the same importance that you give every other element in your business, to put it on par with everything from finance and operations to marketing and customer service.

By changing how you hire, you can generate a ripple effect that will give you a sustainable advantage over your competitors.

"Hiring has always been a bit social and riddled with bias," says William Tincup, the principal at Tincup & Co, and an HR technology analyst and consultant based in Arlington, Texas. "We're not just talking about biases about whether someone has the kind of educational pedigree you want or about race, gender, or sexual orientation. Our biases include work style and a preference for people who work like you do."

Such biases create a homogenous workforce, the antithesis to innovation.

"If you have an inclusive and diverse culture," says Tincup, "you create friction, which creates innovations and leads to greater market share. That's why if we want to make better hiring decisions, we need to come to grip with those biases. Otherwise, we can inadvertently kill our organizations' ability to innovate and compete."

You need to radically rethink how you hire to create an innovative workforce.

Consider what happened at Pillar To Post, a twenty-two-year-old home inspection franchisor with some 536 franchisees spread across forty-eight of the US states and eight Canadian provinces.

"At its core, Pillar To Post is a people business," says founder and CEO Dan Steward. "We make a difference in people's lives by helping them buy a home."

Steward recognized early on that finding and retaining quality inspectors—the company employs about nine hundred of them— was crucial to the success of individual franchises and the company in general.

"The recruitment, selection, and onboarding of good people is the secret sauce in this business," says Steward. "Good people build relationships with customers and real estate agents. When you can establish trust with them, you get more referrals and less price sensitivity."

If Pillar To Post was going to keep up its track record of doubling in size every four years, it needed a steady stream of incoming talent. Yet retention rates throughout the company were just 33 percent. Worse, just one in ten people hired lasted long enough to have a positive effect on the business. These lost employees resulted in enormous amounts of wasted time and resources throughout the company. These added costs made franchise owners exceedingly reluctant to bring on new people, and that created operating issues that cascaded down the rest of the business.

"It was becoming a chokehold on our growth," says Steward. "Poor retention meant we were wasting resources and performing poor quality work that was negatively influencing our brand. If we wanted to build a great company, we needed a clear philosophy on the people side of our business. We realized that there had to be a better way for us to approach hiring."

An added challenge for Steward was that he needed to get his franchisees on board with introducing a new process for recruiting and selecting home inspectors for their individual businesses. Because there was no universal hiring process the company adhered to, every franchise approached hiring in their own way based on their past experiences. The lack of a focused hiring process led to inconsistency and poor results. Steward admits he even made poor decisions with a few key senior-level hires.

"I have come to recognize that it's better to leave a position unfilled than to make a bad hire," he says. "It's easy to look back now and see where I compromised, either on the job requirements, the cultural fit, or the background check. I now appreciate the need to take your time and do it well. If you feel panicked and hire the wrong person just to fill a seat, the cost can be enormous."

"I have come to recognize that it's better to leave a position unfilled than to make a bad hire."

Working together, Steward and his franchise owners revamped how the entire company approached hiring and onboarding.

"We recognized that we needed to all speak the same language and use the same selection tools," says Steward. "We needed to bring some process and discipline to our approach. We had to forget the idea that you can just hire a warm body and hope they work out."

The changes Steward and his team subsequently made to their

hiring process—including rethinking how they interview for things like cultural fit and leveraging their employment brand to attract Millennials (those in the workforce born after 1980)—have had a dramatic influence on the business. Although Steward acknowledges that they still have room to improve, the success rate for new hires has climbed from 10 percent to more than 60 percent. More dramatically, unwanted turnover has dropped to nearly zero. These incredible results have given his franchisees new confidence to increase their hiring. The business is back on the fast track for growth.

"If you aren't focused on your people," says Steward, "you aren't focused on the long-term welfare of your business."

Relearning How to Hire

Most of us are pretty bad at hiring. This shouldn't come as a shock, because the majority of companies don't train managers how to hire well, or at all. Instead, we rely on outdated techniques and gut feelings to make high-impact decisions involving the most valuable assets in our business. Hiring new employees is no different from any other business process. When the process is thought out, documented, and meticulously followed, the results are consistent and produce actionable outcomes. Winging it, on the other hand, produces wide swings in results and no predictability.

Most of us don't prioritize the time it takes to do hiring well. It takes a lot of effort—overall, companies take fifty-two days on average to fill an open position—up from forty-eight days in 2011.[3] During a forty-hour workweek, most managers may be investing less than 10

3   Talent Acquisition Factbook 2015, Bersin by Deloitte/Jennifer Krider, Karen O'Leonard, and Robin Erickson, PhD, April 2015.

percent of their time on hiring. Why is that? The simple answer is that they're beyond busy. They have a job opening to fill and they want to put a checkmark inside that box. But the consequences are too high to continue using this quick approach.

You can't simply delegate the task of hiring to someone else. Even if you're fortunate enough to have a dedicated human resources professional on staff, they are probably bogged down in payroll administration, medical benefits, and training, among many other duties. As much as you'd like them to develop sound hiring practices, you can't count on that happening without getting involved. Ensuring consistency throughout the hiring process needs to be one of your top priorities.

Over the next twenty years, the skill that will separate the mediocre managers from the truly exceptional will be their ability to find, recruit, hire, and retain great people.

Would you rather spend more time up front getting great people in the door, or more time managing the problems created by hiring the wrong people for your organization? The answer should be obvious.

If you can bump up the time you invest in recruiting and hiring to even 20 percent of your week—one day—and employ a clearly defined, consistent hiring process, you can realize a tremendous return on your investment that far exceeds anything else you can do in your business. Over the next twenty years, the skill that will separate the mediocre managers from the truly exceptional will be their ability to find, recruit, hire, and retain great people.

A *hiring process* is the list of steps that take a manager from first understanding and defining a job opening all the way through to a new employee's first day on the job. It's the path that a company starts when it decides that it has a need for a new employee and finishes when the position is filled. Ideally, this process is simple, straightforward, and usable by everyone in your company with minimal training.

I've written this book to teach you a proven, straightforward, and effective method for hiring new employees. In the pages that follow, I will teach you to rethink how you go about finding, assessing, and hiring the best people for your business. By following this process, you will eliminate the guesswork and put yourself back in control of your business.

I've divided the content into four sections that mirror the steps of the hiring process:

Stage One: Define the Role (Chapters 1–2)

In this section, we'll discuss how you need to *define* the kinds of people you're looking for to fill your open positions, which often begins with rethinking your definition of an "ideal candidate." Have you considered, for example, that your next great hire might not have any experience in your industry? Or, that there are four key personality attributes that serve as a near-bulletproof filter for screening high-potential hires? I'll explain what these characteristics are and why they are so important.

Stage Two: Source Your Applicants (Chapter 3)

In this section, we will dig in to how you can *find* the best people. Do you realize that you need to identify at least fifty candidates for every job opening you have to let the mathematics of selection play to your benefit? How on earth can you cast such a wide net? Although most growing businesses rely on popular job sites to push out their job postings, the most successful companies understand that finding great people begins with building your employment brand. When is the last time you went online and looked at your company's job postings? I'll show you why you need to reevaluate your company's employment website.

Stage Three: Select the Right Person (Chapters 4–8)

In this section, you'll learn how to confidently *select* the best potential fits for your organization after you have built up a sizable candidate pool. Picking the right person for the job means you need to go much deeper than a candidate's resume or the fact that they went to the same school as you. In the chapters within this section, I'll share reliable techniques for evaluating candidates through interviews, reference checks, and homework assignments and explain how to win over the best of the best with an offer they can't refuse.

Stage Four: Retain Your Best (Chapter 9)

Employing great people doesn't stop with hiring. In this final section, we'll talk about how you can *keep* your best people with good management practices, including proven onboarding processes and retention techniques.

Don't make the mistake in thinking that the content of this book is just theory. Each section includes case studies from a range of organizations operating in a variety of industries that have renovated their hiring practices using these techniques. You'll also find a set of templates and tools on our website, www.TheBestTeamWins.com /resources, that you can download for free and use to jump-start the revamping of your hiring process. If you have any further questions, join our online community and learn more ways that you can find the best people for your organization.

. . .

CHAPTER SUMMARY

The most valuable asset in your business is your people. They are your true source of sustainable competitive advantage. Most companies are terrible at hiring, which leads to massive costs and business setbacks. The ability to hire and retain great people is the skill that separates the mediocre managers from the truly exceptional. Who you put on your payroll is the only thing you have 100 percent control over in your business. To hire better, you need to relearn how to go about finding, selecting, and retaining great people.

SELF-ANALYSIS

Ask yourself the following questions:

- How did your last bad hire affect your business? Your customers?

- How much time do you invest in the hiring process? Given the stakes involved, is it enough?

- Are you willing to rethink and relearn what it means to hire great people?

KEY TAKEAWAYS

1 Hiring is the one thing you can control in your business, and getting it right provides an immediate return on investment.

2 Hiring is not just a function of HR; you can't delegate it. Every leader needs to incorporate hiring in their daily routine.

3 Investing more time in getting the hiring process right will increase your organization's performance.

Chapter Two

CHANGE YOUR HIRING MINDSET

What if you thought about hiring as if you were selling car insurance? Think about how the car insurance process works: The agent doesn't need to meet you in person to know that if you have a sports car in the garage, four accidents on your driving record, and a sixteen-year-old living under your roof, you're probably going to cost them some money at some point. They've become adept at using historical data to predict the likelihood of certain outcomes, such as you getting into an accident and filing a claim. The riskier you are, the more expensive your policy will be. It's a formula that's been proven over time.

But could you imagine if the insurance underwriter forgot to ask what kind of car you drove when pricing your policy? Or, worse, they didn't bother to check your accident history or discover that you have a teenage driver at home? All those things are crucially important to assessing the risk of a new customer, right? The insurer's risk evaluation processes are designed to uncover these bits of information; it's not by chance that these organizations are good at predicting outcomes.

Business managers can use the same math that big insurers and banks use to determine risk levels and expected outcomes and make better hiring decisions. It's all about scoring factors that will tell you whether there is a higher or a lower likelihood that a candidate will be successful in their new role. So why do you overlook these key risk factors when making your hiring decisions?

When you rewire your thinking along these lines, you'll recognize that the way you've always approached the recruiting and hiring process for your organization is probably not effective at determining which candidate has the best chance of succeeding. If you want to change the quality of people you hire, you need to start by changing what you measure in the selection process. You also need to rethink where your next hire might come from.

Did you know that 50 percent of the factors that predict a person's success or failure in a role have *nothing* to do with their industry experience? In other words, your next great hire is likely to have no experience in whatever business or industry you operate in.

Your next great hire is likely to have no experience in whatever business or industry you operate in.

Clearly, this likelihood has multiple implications for how you go about identifying people to fill your open positions. It also means you can open up ample opportunities to find talent for your organization that your competition might have overlooked. Think of searching for your new hire like how author Michael Lewis described the Oakland A's player scouting and recruiting process in his best-selling book *Moneyball: The Art of Winning an Unfair Game.* The book showed how Billy Beane, the general manager of the A's, was using a different lens to evaluate players who were overlooked by other clubs.

Working for a team with a limited budget, Beane couldn't just go out and sign every high-priced free agent (or even keep many of his own high-priced players). He needed an edge—something that would help him identify players he could afford who could also perform on the field. Unlike traditional scouts, who valued whether a player "looked like a major leaguer," Beane and his team of Ivy League–educated assistants dug in to statistics such as on-base percentage to find players who might not look the part but could perform. His now-famous results have become something of baseball legend; he crafted the Athletics into one of the most cost-effective teams in base-ball. For example, in the 2006 MLB season, the Athletics ranked twen-ty-fourth of thirty major league teams in player salaries but had the fifth-best regular-season record.

So how do you go about identifying potential players for your organization? Have you found a way to identify talent overlooked by your competitors? Take a lesson from Billy Beane, and look beyond the metrics everyone else uses. For you, this means looking beyond someone's resume.

It's no longer good enough to rely on someone's resume to deter-mine if they would make a good hire. *Resumes are marketing docu-ments.* They're designed to land an interview. Resumes don't tell you anything about how the candidate performs to expectations or how well they might fit in your culture. And yet, most companies make a candidate's resume the cornerstone of their hiring process. We have established that your people are your business's most valuable resource and that the cost of making bad hires is enormous. Doesn't it seem to be awfully risky to rely heavily on a person's resume—something that is clearly biased to make them look their best—to make one of the most important decisions for your business?

Case Study: Look for People
Outside Your Industry

Joe Turchyn has a unique perspective on the automotive retail business. With a background in investment banking and finance firms like E. F. Hutton, Turchyn is now the director of corporate development and strategy of a car dealership in New Jersey. Turchyn was lured into the car business by his brother-in-law, a former finance executive who had originally bought the dealership, when his brother-in-law asked for Turchyn's advice on buying some data mining software. When he began studying the industry, Turchyn realized how much the automotive retail business was being disrupted by technology—especially when it came to the people needed to run the business.

Turchyn learned that the dealership needed people on staff who would be able to get the most out of the data mining software.

"You need to have the skill set on hand of how to understand the ups and downs of the software," says Turchyn. "You also have to think about how it integrates and talks to everything else in your business."

When Turchyn looked inside his own dealership, he saw that it had forty different vendors it bought services from—none of which were well integrated with each other.

Turchyn began to realize that if his dealership was going to survive the disruption caused by the proliferation of technology—and thrive— they needed to rethink the kind of skill sets necessary for their staff.

"The entire business is changing," he says. "Soon, the showroom will look different because of technologies like mobile and cloud computing. The process of buying cars needs to change. Customers don't want to be shuffled from the sales office to finance office inside the dealership like they have always been. Consumers hate it. They want simple and convenient, not high pressure."

But where could Turchyn find the people with the skill sets he was looking for who could also embrace that kind of change?

"The answer was that we needed to attract people from outside our industry who have never developed the bad habits we're trying to avoid," he says. "We need to attract young people who have passion, not the people who have been recycled from job to job and from dealer to dealer."

Turchyn and his business partner made the decision to leverage process and technology to help attract people to his dealership who might never have considered working in the automotive industry before. Turchyn and his partner focused on selling the "cool" factor of the industry and the opportunity to pursue a true career path and pursued candidates that were untraditional. Case in point: He was excited by the potential of one candidate, a young woman about to graduate college. This candidate worked at her school's newspaper documenting sporting events via video, photo, and social media posts.

Where would a person with those skills fit inside a car dealership, of all places?

Turchyn thinks someone like that could fill a number of roles, including a new position called *delivery coordinator*. If you were to buy a car from a traditional dealership, it is the job of your salesperson to help walk you through the bells and whistles of your new purchase once you have completed the transaction—what insiders call *delivery*—a process that can take upward of an hour.

But Turchyn began to ask, "Why would you want your top salespeople delivering cars and not selling more of them?"

Now, if Turchyn could bring on this new hire with good technology, social media skills, and good communication and time management chops, he could position her in a central post inside the dealership, where she could deliver cars and put those skills to use.

"One of the happiest times in someone's life is when they first take a seat in their new car," says Turchyn. "We should be taking their picture or shooting a video of them and putting that up on social media. We can then help the customer put up a review on Yelp, making it easy for them to do that right then and there."

Turchyn says this is just one example of a job that doesn't exist in his market, but could emerge as the nature of auto showrooms changes in the future. Another thing certain to change is where he looks for his next great employees—outside his industry.

"In today's tech world, everyone tries to position their product or service as a platform," says Turchyn. "But the human capital platform is where you get your true leverage. That's where you can do something special."

Rethinking Your Investment

Hiring is all about risk assessment. In fact, we can define *hiring* as the process of assessing the potential risk of a candidate *not* being able to achieve the outcomes that you need them to with the resources you're providing. When you make the decision to hire someone, you take a calculated risk that they will become a productive member of your organization. Unfortunately, there will never be a foolproof and risk-free way to evaluate candidates. But if you could increase the odds from a coin flip where you have a mere 50 percent chance of getting the right answer, to a more sure bet of 70 percent or even 80 percent chance you're making the right hire, wouldn't that be worth the extra time and effort?

If you ever watch professional poker players, this is exactly how they think: It's all about expected value. The *expected value* of a decision is the sum of all the possible outcomes resulting from that decision multiplied by the likelihood that each of those outcomes would occur. It's an educated bet based on the odds of certain outcomes happening.

In simple terms, the expected value of a coin flip is zero over the long run. If you flip a coin a thousand times, it will theoretically yield five hundred heads and five hundred tails. There's no advantage to picking heads or tails; it's a wash. If you invested $1,000,000 in heads, after one thousand coin flips you're going to be at even money. But consider what would happen if you could rig that coin flip to come up heads six or seven times out of ten? You'd have an investment guaranteed to yield substantial profits over the long run.

To use the betting analogy, a poker player typically weighs the decision of whether or not to play their hand against their opponent based on two factors: their starting hand and the size of the pot. When you have a great starting hand, you bet big because your great hand is likely to beat everyone else's hand. You can't expect to win every hand, but you will generate positive returns over the long run despite the occasional miss, because you bet your chips when the expected value of that decision is positive. A series of decisions made with a positive expected value will yield a positive result, even though you'll lose some along the way.

Now back to our discussion of hiring as risk assessment. If you look back on your results hiring salespeople for your business and determine that you have a 40 percent success rate, that means six out of ten hires you make fail to deliver the expected result. If, for simplicity's sake, one rep costs $100,000 per year, you're pushing $1 million of your capital into the pot. Your expected value calculation based on this history would tell you that you're going to lose $600,000 of that money due to bad hires (60 percent of $1 million).

To expand on this example, let's say that a successful rep produces $200,000 their first year in new revenue and that a poor rep produces zero. Your expected value for hiring those ten reps is as follows:

$800,000 [4 successful reps × $200,000 of revenue]
− $1 million [10 total reps × $100,000 of cost
per rep] = −$200,000 expected value.

Losing $200,000 doesn't sound like much fun to me.

But what if you were able to get the hiring decision right seven times out of ten? You just increased your expected value to a positive $400,000—a pretty incredible result, wouldn't you agree? Let's look at that math:

$1.4 million [7 successful reps × $200,000 of
revenue] − $1 million [10 total reps × $100,000
of cost per rep] = $400,000 expected value.

FIG 2.1—POOR HIRING RESULTS ARE EXPENSIVE

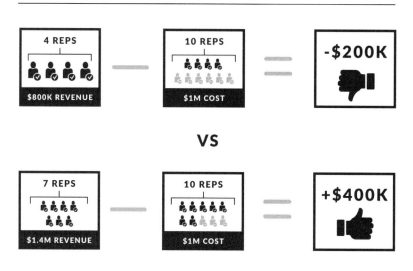

There, that feels better.

Most managers just blindly hire sales reps, hoping that they'll work out. Given the high stakes that we just outlined, it's a much safer bet to let a position go unfilled than to hire someone who isn't a fit. *It's better to have an empty seat than a bad hire.* The cost of being wrong is just too great.

Now that we have established that hiring is the process of assessing risk, how can we go about looking at talent in a fresh new *Moneyball* kind of way? How do we know what the expected outcomes will be?

The answer is by assessing how someone scores on the four Super Elements.

Introducing the Super Elements

Ever since companies have been hiring employees, employers have been trying to figure out how to predict employee fit. Sure, you'd like everyone you hire to be a go-getter and to have a likable personality, but do these traits predict how successful a candidate will be in a given job?

In a word: no. They don't. Neither does the fact that the candidate went to your *alma mater* or likes the same sports team you do. No matter how much you might like someone, it doesn't predict that they will be good at their job. You have to rewire your brain to suspend your gut feelings, because they're the reason you keep making poor hiring decisions.

But there is good news: There is a way to screen candidates for a job that shifts the odds back in your favor. If we're searching for someone who has a high likelihood of succeeding in a given job, there are elements that we must score to make that determination—competency levels, certain behavioral traits, and vocational or technical skills, for example. At Hireology, we call these things the *Elements of Success*.

Our research shows that these measurements—attitude, accountability, past related-job success, and cultural fit—are the most significant predictors of job performance, across every type of job. These four measurable elements are so highly predictive that a manager needs to only focus on these four factors to consistently improve their hiring results. We call these factors the Super Elements. Organizations that find ways to measure these Super Elements in their interview processes are more likely to hire people who will succeed in their jobs. If a candidate scores well on all four of these measures, you have a high-potential hire.

Attitude

In the Super Elements, *attitude* is defined as a person's disposition toward work. If your candidate has a positive disposition toward the act of working, then they have a "positive attitude." Research shows that outside of an intermittent "case of the Mondays," a person's satisfaction with their job stays relatively stable over time—including when they change jobs or companies. This finding implies that there is something innate in a person that predisposes them to report a positive (or negative) attitude toward their work.

According to one fascinating research project conducted at the University of Minnesota, we are hardwired with either a positive or negative attitude toward work. The study involved thirty-four pairs of identical twins who had been separated from each other when they were, on average, six months old. They were not reunited until they were thirty-two years old. The researchers asked the twins to answer a questionnaire to study how heredity affected job satisfaction. The participants reported coming from a wide range of careers that included housewife, research chemist, coal miner, assembly line worker, computer analyst, machinist, nurse, and financial planner.

The researchers learned that after they controlled for every external variable they could think of—the gender of the two twins, whether they were married or had kids, where they lived—the attitude that each twin had toward their job was *exactly the same* as their sibling.

Richard Arvey, the industrial psychologist who ran the study, concluded that genes might be part of the reason some people seem happy no matter what they do, whereas others have trouble finding a satisfying job.[4] This finding is supported by similar research on twins conducted in Finland, which showed that our genes might also influence a person's job choice, satisfaction with life, and frequency of changing jobs. Our job satisfaction might be hardwired in our DNA.

Now combine this amazing idea with other research that tells us employees who have a positive attitude are more productive, helpful,

4   Malcolm Ritter, "Remarkable Similarities Found in Those Reared Apart: Study of Identical Twins Links Genes to Job Satisfaction," *Los Angeles Times,* May 7, 1989.

and likely to stay at their jobs.[5] If we agree that positive attitudes lead to better outcomes at work, doesn't it make sense to screen for a positive attitude when we hire?

There are numerous approaches to measure employee attitude. A quick example might be asking a candidate to describe the most frustrating aspect of their prior job. Ask them what makes it harder for them to do their job. If the person tells you, for example, they worked for a manager who had a different working style that made it hard for them to get along and that they look at this new position as one where they will be able to learn and grow, consider that a positive spin on things. Conversely, if the candidate tells you that their manager was "a total jerk" and "had no idea about what they were doing," well . . . you get the idea.

Because job satisfaction is stable across time (it is predicted by a person's disposition) and because job satisfaction is linked to good performance, we can reasonably assume that a candidate who recalls a positive outlook on past experiences will likely be a better performer—no matter what the job might be.

Accountability

The extent to which a person believes they have control over their own outcomes is what industrial psychologists call their *locus of control*. When good or bad things happen, does the person take accountability for their actions and for their contribution to that result? In psychology parlance, there are two loci—an internal locus of control and an external locus of control.

---

5   Robert J. Vance, "Employee Engagement and Commitment: A Guide to Understanding, Measuring, and Increasing Engagement in Your Organization," SHRM Foundation, 2006, https://www.shrm.org/about/foundation/research/Documents/1006EmployeeEngagementOnlineReport.pdf.

Research tells us that people with an internal locus of control tend to perform better at their jobs across all roles. Specifically, people who feel that they have direct control over their environment perform significantly better than those who attribute personal outcomes to external factors such as other individuals, luck, or fate. People with an internal locus of control will attribute the events that happen in their job—both good and bad—to their own actions or decisions, whereas people with an external locus of control will tend to make excuses.

It's simple to determine which camp your job candidate falls into. In the interview, ask your candidate about the last time they set a goal for themselves that they failed to achieve. The pronouns they use can be extremely illuminating. If they answer with statements like "*I* could have done a better job planning this effort," or "*I* should have realized that my decision would lead to issues," they likely have an internal locus of control. On the other hand, if they blame the economy or their manager—"It wasn't my fault!"—you know they likely have an external locus of control. When a candidate places the blame on external factors, you should see a red flag.

Past Related-Job Success

We have already explained that someone's experience in a particular industry has a limited bearing on how well they will perform for you. Still, researchers have generally accepted that past behavior is the most accurate predictor of future behavior. Behavior-based interviews (a regular practice in many organizations) are modeled around this assumption. Accordingly, the interviewer asks questions about how the candidate performed certain tasks in the past that they will also be required to do, if they are hired, in the future. Although conducting behavior-based interviews is valuable, they require careful research of the specific behaviors you hope to see on the job. The term *past behavior* is too general to be considered a universally predictive element. The term *past related-job success* is, however, a better universal predictor of future job success.

A candidate has past related-job success if they have met formal goals in past jobs that are similar to the goals of the job they are applying for. If the context of the person's past job—activities, goals, and environment—closely matches the context of the job you are hiring them for, a candidate who met or exceeded their goals in the past job is likely to meet or achieve similar goals in the future.

A great example of this dynamic emerges when you evaluate someone who has been successful in a highly structured role in specialty retail, such as a car dealership or a restaurant. Anyone who has ever had the opportunity to work as a barista at a place like Starbucks can tell you with incredible detail how every minute of their shift was monitored and measured. Average customer wait times, average ticket price, drink refunds, and wastage are just some of the many metrics of their performance. A person who succeeds in this environment is more likely to succeed in a role that requires them to manage themselves to hourly targets like customer wait times.

On the flip side, hiring someone who has never had their performance actively monitored or measured doesn't guarantee that they're going to fail to achieve the desired result. It just means the risk that they'll fail to achieve the desired result is higher, because they've never worked in a similar work environment. Thus, over the long run, the expected value of hiring people who have never been managed this way is lower than people who have been measured to specific outcomes.

To screen for past related-job success in a candidate, a direct approach is best: Ask them about a job where their success was measured. Ask them to describe the metrics by which their work was measured on a daily or weekly basis. Then, ask how they performed relative to their peers. You'll learn a lot from how they answer this question. If your candidate says their performance has never been tracked or if they give you weak answers that are light on details, you know they fail to meet this standard.

Cultural Fit

Cultural fit is the degree to which the job applicant shares similar values with the organization and demonstrates an authentic interest in the job at hand. Admittedly, screening for someone who is a cultural fit with your organization is a bit of a gray area. Defining your company's culture is challenging, and it can be difficult to use the description of your culture in a hiring context.

To help you define your company culture, you may want to try the "Mission to Mars" exercise. Coined by renowned business guru Jim Collins in his classic book *Built to Last*, the idea is to imagine that we are sending a mission to the red planet to meet with newly discovered alien life forms. You get to pick who we send to serve as the representatives of all of humanity. You have to pick the best person in your company to send, and you can't send yourself. Who would you send? Why did you pick that person specifically? What qualities do they demonstrate that you feel are exemplary of your culture? Is it because they show up on time? Or is it because they ruthlessly make their numbers? Maybe it is because they are kind and quick to help others.

The words and descriptions that end up on that list are what you, as a manager, value in an employee; they're *your* core values. When you're looking for new talent, it's important to screen candidates to see if the values that motivate them, the *how* of what they do, are a match for you and the company.

Another potential red flag to watch for is whether the candidate actually wants the job. It's worth understanding where the person stands in their job hunt and, if the job was offered to them, whether they would take it. Or, if they did take the job, would it be as a placeholder and a paycheck while they keep looking for that perfect gig? Knowing the answer to this question can save you a lot of time and aggravation.

Evaluating this candidate's fit with your organization takes the guesswork out of hiring; it isn't a coin flip anymore. You have an edge in placing your bet and are greatly reducing the riskiness of the hire.

Case Study: Prioritize Cultural Fit over Experience

As a serial entrepreneur who has cofounded five high-growth businesses over his career, Michael Krasman has done his fair share of hiring. He is currently the cofounder and CEO of UrbanBound, a cloud-based relocation-management software company.

In guiding fast-growth companies, Krasman knows firsthand how challenging it can be to fill open positions with qualified candidates.

"You can reach a point of desperation in trying to fill a role," he says.

But disaster can strike if you hire someone who isn't a fit for your organization.

"Making sure people will fit in your company culture is paramount to being successful," Krasman says.

A company isn't your building or your stock price; it's a group of people coming together to solve problems.

"Your culture is the culmination of the people you choose to hire,"

Krasman says. "It will evolve based on the people you bring to the company. That's why it's so important to guard your hiring decisions."

There will be times when you need to say no to hiring someone even when they seem to match all the skills and experience you think you're looking for.

Case in point: Krasman recalls the early days at one of his companies when they were looking to hire a top-notch salesperson. He felt lucky when they identified someone who had everything they were looking for.

"He had an unbelievably vast Rolodex of contacts in the areas we were looking to expand to," says Krasman. They hired him.

But the salesman's experience had come from large corporations that had far more infrastructure and resources than the start-up he had just joined.

"We sort of ignored that he had never worked in our kind of environment before," says Krasman.

After three months, it was clear that their new sales hire was struggling to adapt to the fast-moving culture that his new company demanded. "He just couldn't or wouldn't make the adjustment," says Krasman, who was forced to let the salesperson go.

It was an expensive lesson for Krasman. But one of the payoffs is that he now prioritizes time during interviews to explain to candidates what it means to work in a fast-paced environment and what would be expected of them to thrive within it.

Hiring for cultural fit isn't a static exercise either.

"You have to keep evaluating the business as it keeps growing," Krasman says. "The culture of a start-up is very different from that of a company celebrating its tenth anniversary. It's a natural evolution, and the people you hire have to match the needs you have at that time."

Entrepreneurs can fall into a trap, though, when they get stuck thinking about hiring for the company they want to have in the future instead of hiring for the needs and culture they have right now.

"You want to hire that superstar seasoned executive who is capable of running a very complicated operation," says Krasman. "But if you are only ten people in a room, that person might not be a fit for the challenges you actually face today."

Getting Specific

Starting your recruiting process without properly defining the job is akin to driving a car at night with your headlights turned off—you might get where you're trying to go, but you're just as likely to crash the car. That's where the job profile comes in. A *job profile* is a document that describes the business reasons for the position you are hiring for and the results that must be achieved by the new employee during their first twelve months in order for them to be considered successful.

A job profile is more than the typical job description that you're used to writing. Take a moment to dig out the last job description that you used to fill an open position in your company. Does it list requirements like "good interpersonal communication skills" and "works well with others in a team environment"? Does it list educational requirements like "bachelor's degree required, advanced degree a plus"? Does it rattle off ambiguous activities like "make cold calls" or "develop new relationships with prospects"—or, better yet, "provide excellent customer service"? How about the perennial favorite, "Must have at least [X] years of experience in either [Y] role or in the [Z] industry"?

You probably answered, "Yep, sure does" to one of those questions. That's okay. Managers are rarely trained how to write good job descriptions. An entrepreneur or manager rarely has access to truly top-notch coaching on this topic. Most managers just give it their best shot. They write a job description that details the basic outline of the job duties and typically describe 90 percent of everyone in the potential candidate pool—good and bad performers alike.

I mean, who *doesn't* want someone who works well with others? You don't see job descriptions that say, "Will consider people who, on occasion, act like total jerks."

Thinking about the Role

Try doing something differently. Lay out what you want this job to be and what you expect your future employee to do for your business. Defining things such as your desired candidate's experience, responsibilities, expectations for customer interaction and travel, and required skills will help you better structure your entire process. Keep the following in mind as you begin to define the position:

- Use job descriptions that clearly define your open positions and that attract qualified candidates.

- Think about what kind of experience you want to set for your candidates throughout the entire hiring process.

- Analyze your expectations and requirements for your open job.

- Think about what kind of behavioral and skills testing you want your candidates to complete in your selection process.

- Remember to think about the salary, benefits, and any other perks you'll be offering to your future employees.

- Consider your company culture and organizational structure in addition to basic job requirements.

After you have considered all of the requirements in this list, you are ready to start defining the role.

First, make a list of everything that you think this person will be responsible for on a daily and weekly basis. For example, if the position being considered is a sales role, daily activities might be things including "make cold calls to potential clients" and "create pricing proposals for delivery to prospects." Weekly activities would be things like "submit sales pipeline report" and "update CRM system." We're not getting too detailed at this point but are painting a general picture of the new role to spot-check the result for glaring inconsistencies or issues.

Next, write down all of the reasons you think the position is justifiable from an economic standpoint. Because we're all about getting a return on our investment, we want to make sure that the investment in this position is going to yield positive results—in the form of revenue, cost savings, or efficiency and productivity gains.

Although this two-step approach to defining the role is by no means a groundbreaking one, it never ceases to amaze me how many people launch right into writing a job description without pausing to consider the validity of the opening that they are going to create. Don't allow yourself to skip these crucial steps, because it can cost you dearly once you're too far in the hiring process. Either you'll realize that you're looking for the wrong type of person and have to start over from scratch, or you'll hire someone that you don't need and waste your money.

Both results are bad.

Writing a Job Profile

Creating a job profile begins with asking the question, "Why am I creating this new position?" This is what I call the *position background*. Your response should answer the following questions:

- What is the primary business driver that justifies this position in my company or team?
- Is this a new position or a replacement or modification of an existing role?
- If someone was in this role before, what factors led to their success or lack thereof?

Once you've defined the position background and are comfortable with your answers, it's time to move to the next step: "defining success."

At this point, we ask the question, "Looking out twelve months, what things will this person have had to accomplish in order for me to consider them successful in this role?"

The answer should be specific and based on metrics or numbers so that they are devoid of any subjective criteria.

For a sales role, these may be outcomes such as the following:

- Generate $500,000 in revenue from new clients.
- Follow up on all marketing leads within 24 hours of receipt and obtain a close rate of 30 percent from those leads.
- Expand existing territory from $150,000 to $450,000 within the first year of employment.

For a controller role, some examples might be:

- Reduce days sales outstanding (DSO) to fewer than fifty within the first six months of employment.

- Build a twelve-month cash flow projection tool within the first three months of employment.

- Migrate the company from QuickBooks to NetSuite by the end of the third quarter.

The theme here is specificity. We want to communicate the requirements of the job by using the desired result as our starting point. We can then use these criteria throughout the interview process to find out whether a particular candidate has ever delivered results that are similar to those we're looking for in the open role. We want to avoid ambiguous requirements like "initiate new client relationships" (okay, how many?) or "deliver excellent customer service" (as measured by what?). If you find that you don't have the foggiest idea what metrics to use, *don't hire anyone yet*. Better to stop the process, think it through, and proceed after you know what the result should be.

Having specific results in mind as you write a job profile is powerful because it's great for identifying and preventing three common issues:

1. No Financial Justification for the Position

In many cases, an entrepreneur or manager thought they needed someone, but when they tried to articulate why on paper, it didn't make financial sense. If you don't have financial justification, either figure out how to get more value out of the role, or redistribute the work to your current staff more efficiently.

2. Not Enough Work for the Role

Another common result at this point is realizing that you don't have enough work to allocate to this newly defined role. Many managers end up with a job opening that requires twenty to thirty hours per week, and therefore can't justify adding a full-time position. Faced with the prospect of two part-time yet seemingly crucial roles, many managers opt to create a hybrid role—something I like to call a *tweener*. This is usually a bad idea, for reasons we'll discuss shortly. Avoid the tweeners!

3. Too Much Work for the Role

This is a case of having ten pounds of job in a five-pound bag. After you've created a list of daily and weekly activities, it's clear that no human could accomplish them all. You've crammed every conceivable need in this one position, making a monstrous *Frankenjob* that dooms its hapless creator to greater misery. It's possible that you may need to divide the role into multiple positions, particularly if you've put off hiring over a long period of time because of financial constraints. If you can justify two or more new roles financially, then do it! You'll be glad you did.

The Tweener—Avoid at All Costs!

When you combine two seemingly compatible but different part-time roles into one full-time role, you've created a tweener. Tweeners are bad.

An entrepreneur friend of mine who runs an incredibly successful apparel company called to ask my opinion of a new position he was looking to fill.

"So, what kind of role are you envisioning?" I asked him.

"Well," starts my CEO friend, "I'm looking for a *controller slash office manager*, someone who can handle our accounting needs and manage the day-to-day administrative functions of the company. I'm thinking of it as a hybrid role for someone who is good at both things."

We all know where this story ends. This entrepreneur, having the limited resources typical of most early-stage firms, makes the decision to combine two seemingly similar roles into one position.

"Accounting is an administrative function," went this CEO's thought process, "so I can also offload all of this office management crap that I'm dealing with by giving it to the new controller. And because I don't think I have forty hours a week's worth of either accounting work or administrative management work to perform, I can get a twofer with this hybrid position. Problem solved."

Problem created, actually.

By combining the controller need with the office manager need, this CEO created a tweener—a dual role that combines two similar but vastly different positions in an attempt to get more value out of a new position. It makes perfect sense, right? Get maximum productive yield out of each salary dollar spent. But it's rife with risk, because inherent in this decision is an increased risk the person hired will lack star performance potential in *either* role, resulting in someone who underperforms in *both* roles.

Entrepreneurs wear a hundred different hats each and every day—salesperson, HR manager, controller, stamp licker—and they have the mental wiring and skill set to pull off each of them in the early days of the company. But that doesn't mean future employees of the firm will be anywhere near as adept at keeping the plates spinning. Most entrepreneurs assume that the rest of the world operates with the same ability to jump tracks and multitask on disparate projects. It's just not the case.

People who make great entrepreneurs usually make fairly terrible employees. People who are superstar employees became superstars because they're exceptional at one thing—being a controller, being a sales manager, being a human resources generalist. Perhaps they can function in other areas, but I'm going to bet that they're much better at one thing than any of the others.

As a business leader, it's *your* job to decide what kind of role you need to fill. When you fail to isolate a single job description, you make it nearly impossible to find a resource that will have a high likelihood of success when they start to work for you. You're risking throwing months of high-dollar salary into a deep hole. Failing to make up your mind can be expensive.

Figure out what you *really* need. If you don't have enough work to make the new job a full-time role, make it a part-time role. Outsource it. Do it yourself for a little longer while you try to figure out your single most important need.

Case Study: Define What You're Looking For up Front

Cathi Trippe has worked for Phil Long, a Colorado car dealership with thirteen franchises, for the past twenty years. When she originally joined the company, she was the director of risk management, where she oversaw areas such as worker's compensation and the company's insurance plans. But in the wake of the US economic recession of 2008, Trippe's company was forced to lay off nearly half its workforce, cutting it from 1,500 people to 790—an experience that was "soul crushing," says Trippe.

Trippe's role then evolved as she was asked to head up human resources, where her risk management skills proved valuable. Although she was new to an HR role, she saw opportunities to make positive changes in how the business went about hiring people as the economy began to improve. She also saw the risks that came hand in hand with making poor hiring decisions. In particular, she zeroed in on the company's high turnover rate, which was about 80 percent for frontline workers, in part because of the downsizing they had just been through.

"I wanted to know why people were leaving us," says Trippe. "I wanted to know where we were weak and where we could improve."

Trippe researched how her company had hired in the past and realized that when a hiring manager lost someone, they automatically looked to fill that position rather than using it as an opportunity to evaluate whether there was a real need for it.

"There was just a knee-jerk reaction to fill a hole [rather than] understanding what the real need was," says Trippe.

Using this insight, Trippe then implemented a new process in which she would interview hiring managers and coach them to define who they needed for a position and why they needed it before they began looking for candidates.

"The most crucial change we made was asking questions before we placed an ad for a job out of habit," says Trippe.

Did the manager need someone for just lube and filter changes at $14 an hour, for example, or was the real need for a diesel technician at $30 an hour?

The results have more than validated the changes Trippe has implemented. As the workforce of the company has climbed back to the one-thousand-employee mark, turnover has dropped to less than 50 percent. But Trippe's ultimate goal is to drop turnover even lower, to 36 percent, by treating hiring more like risk management. Thanks to Trippe's changes in the hiring process, this goal is within the company's grasp.

The Hiring Process: a Preview

Now that you've rethought the kinds of people you want to fill your open positions, it's time to talk about how you actually go about finding and hiring them. Here is the five-step hiring process we'll be digging into over the next few chapters:

Step 1: Candidate Sourcing

During this step, the recruiter uses a combination of tools, technology, and networking techniques (not to mention some good ol' fashioned cold calling) to locate candidates who, based on either their current job title or resume, appear to fit the requirements of the open position. The manager either emails or phones the candidate to determine the candidate's interest and availability. The most promising ones move to step two.

Step 2: Initial Interviews

This step is the first real interaction with the candidates during an initial telephone interview. These interviews last anywhere from fifteen minutes to an hour, depending on the type of role. Roughly 75 percent of the candidates found in step one are eliminated in step two. We'll discuss this step in much more detail elsewhere. The remaining 25 percent of the initial candidate pool moves on.

Step 3: In-Person Interviews

Face-to-face interviews are scheduled between the candidates and the hiring manager. Other members of the company may be present at these interviews, depending on their role and the hiring process. Each person questions the candidates. Typically, around 50 percent of the candidates are eliminated at this step. The finalists (around 10 percent of the original step one pool) move on to a second round of in-person interviews.

Step 4: Assessments, References, and Background Checks

Here, we're talking about skills and job-fit assessments. The hiring manager will also call the final candidates' previous managers to determine whether they performed to expectations in their previous roles and to confirm the information that the candidates conveyed during interviews. After this step, you should have a clear front-runner for the role. That person gets moved to step five.

Step 5: Make an Offer

In the final step, the hiring manager delivers an offer package for the winning candidate to review.

Now that you have a sense of how the process flows, it's time to get the word out to possible applicants.

• • •

CHAPTER SUMMARY

At its core, hiring is an exercise in risk management. Yet most companies are wildly underprepared when it comes to their hiring processes. They rely too much on the information on a candidate's resume or on their personal connections to make hiring decisions. These decisions expose them to huge risks through bad hires. The cost of a bad hire is enormous, but you can realize tremendous returns in your organization by increasing your efficacy.

You need to rethink how you hire and what your ideal candidates represent. Your next great hire might come from a completely different industry. You should look for the most significant predictors of job performance, across every job type—the Super Elements: attitude, a sense of accountability, past related-job success, and cultural fit. The organizations that measure these four Super Elements in their interview processes are more likely to hire people who will succeed in their jobs.

Many hiring managers fail to define the job they are looking to fill. They do nothing more than write up a job description. Great hiring decisions begin with a well-crafted job profile that clearly defines what a new hire will be doing the first day and beyond.

SELF-ANALYSIS

Ask yourself the following questions:

- When was the last time you documented and evaluated your hiring process?

- Who makes the final hiring decisions in your organization? Is there a process or a set of objective criteria they use to make that decision?

- How often do you make the time and effort to define the job you are trying to fill *before* you start looking to fill it?

KEY TAKEAWAYS

I   Treat your hiring process like an insurance company treats underwriting a new policy: Assess the risks. Understand what you need to know to reduce the risk of making a bad hire.

2   Rethink the profiles of the people you are recruiting by looking beyond their resume and work history. Look for people with

the four Super Elements that match what you need in your organization.

Make the time up front to create a job profile of the position you want to fill. Only after you've completed your job profile should you begin looking to fill it.

SOURCE YOUR APPLICANTS

Chapter Three

FIND THE RIGHT CANDIDATES

You've nailed down the kind of people you want to hire. You know what you're hiring them to do. Now it's time to tackle how you go about attracting people to your open positions.

William Tincup, HR technology analyst and principal of Tincup & Co, sees a fatal flaw in most recruiting approaches. "A typical business owner or manager doesn't recruit new employees; they hire them," says Tincup. "We've taken the fun out of hiring. It should be an exciting, fun process because we're adding someone to the team that can take us to the next level. Instead of making it fun, we've made it hard."

Regardless of what kind of business you are in, hiring for any role—from sales associate to CEO—comes down to making a match between the company and the candidate based on culture, skills, and competencies.

"A lot of hiring boils down to whether you can establish trust and respect," Tincup says. "No one ever left a company where they felt trusted and respected."

A key part of an employment brand is being honest—good or bad—about what your organization's culture revolves around. Your message might not appeal to everyone, but that's a good thing. You are only trying to attract the people who match your culture. Tincup points to the story of Amazon, which drew a lot of flack from the media in 2016 over the portrayal of its hard-charging and demanding work culture. But the journalists made a mistake in their narrative when they negatively judged Amazon.

"It wasn't that Amazon had a bad culture," Tincup says. "It was just their culture. If you don't like it, then you don't have to work there. If you don't want to work a hundred hours a week, it's not the place for you."

The more transparent you are about who you are as an organization, the easier it will be to attract candidates who connect with your culture. The worst outcome is when someone gets in the door and feels like you lied to them.

"Just tell the truth," says Tincup, "and you've already increased your odds of success in your next hire."

Managers tend to focus on the pain of having to restart their candidate search from scratch and discount the pain that will occur if they hire someone who's unqualified or a bad cultural fit. It takes a minimum of three viable finalist candidates—ones who have made it through the selection process to the final step—to yield a single successful hire.

> **It takes a minimum of three viable finalist candidates—ones who have made it through the selection process to the final step—to yield a single successful hire.**

Don't fall into the trap of having to choose between your one viable candidate and the option of letting the position go unfilled.

Most entrepreneurs and managers don't have a good handle on the sheer volume of work it takes to produce three to five viable finalists for an open position. To better understand the effort involved, let's work backward from your goal: a *minimum of three* viable final candidates.

It typically takes at least three candidates who have come through the in-person interview stage to yield a finalist. So, to get three finalists, you need to interview at least *nine* people in person.

It typically takes three telephone interviews to yield a candidate who's qualified, interested, available in your role, and whom you will invite in for an interview. So, to get nine in-person interviews, you need to conduct *twenty-seven* initial telephone interviews.

It typically takes five resumes to find one candidate who qualifies for a telephone screen. So, to get twenty-seven telephone screens, you need to review approximately *130* resumes.

Finding 130 resumes to review—that's the problem we need to solve.

fig 3.1—Candidate Recruitment Funnel

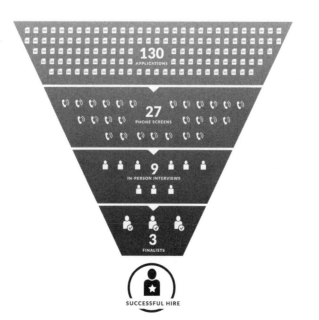

Although your first inclination might be to start posting to major job boards, you might be overlooking the most valuable tool for attracting top talent—your employment brand.

Case Study: Hiring for Cultural Fit

"When it comes to understanding who you are hiring for a role on your team, it's crucial to understand how the culture of your organization will influence that role," says Candice Crane.

Crane is a principal at Crane Automotive, a human resource consultancy to the auto industry based in Atlanta.

Crane, who began her career after graduating from the prestigious Enterprise Rent-a-Car management-training program, says that prioritizing cultural fit needs to be dynamic, particularly if your organization is spread across multiple locations.

"The culture of each location could be different," she says. "Even if you are hiring positions that have the same title in multiple places, you have to understand what differences are in place before you make your decision. You can't recruit the same person across the board."

It's important to understand who would be attracted to a particular position—and who wouldn't.

For example, Crane worked with an auto dealership that had multiple locations that each sold a different brand of car. This changing variable meant that when the business went to hire salespeople, they needed to understand the different cultures in each store as part of the hiring process. These different cultures could mean a change in how people communicate, the sales focus of their business model, or the customers the brand attracts. In the past, the business hadn't made those distinctions clear to candidates and just hired to fill open positions without thinking whether that person would be a cultural fit or not.

Ultimately, Crane coached her client to explain the different cultures involved with each of their stores during the interview process. This change helped candidates to self-select the stores that appealed to them.

"We found that when we took the time to explain the cultural differences to candidates, they could rank where they wanted to work," says Crane. "This immediately helped us make better hires and retain employees longer."

Building a Strong Employment Brand

Most companies spend a fortune building their business brand. In the hypercompetitive world we live in, your brand is one of the most valuable assets you control. A strong *brand* establishes the credibility, goodwill, and trust that buyers want when they purchase your product or service.

What about your *employment brand*? An employment brand is how your local market's talent pool perceives your organization as a potential employer. Make no mistake—you're competing with other businesses for the best talent. Just like a strong brand sets you apart in a retail store or business-to-business marketplace, a strong employment brand differentiates you from your competition when it comes to landing the best job candidates. Conversely, if you employ a weak or even nonexistent employment brand, it's almost a guarantee that you'll be interviewing your competitors' cast-offs.

The best example of your employment brand is your career website. These days, people do just about everything online. This is especially true when it comes to shopping for new products and services. Customers of all kinds use your website to gauge whether or not to purchase from you. Did you realize that people are doing the exact same thing when considering whether or not to apply to your open job?

You've probably invested significant time and money getting your website to a point where it's producing leads. Your career site needs the same attention to attract great job candidates. A great career site directly affects the quality of job applicants, and it has real financial consequences. Chances are that you're spending a lot of money on job boards and employment ads, but you can't recoup that investment if you're not directing those leads to a strong career site that speaks to your candidate pool.

To see an example of what I'm talking about, the website for Schomp Automotive in Denver, Colorado, absolutely nails it. Check out one of the best career sites in the auto industry at http://careers .schomp.com.

What Does Your Employment Brand Look Like?

If you're wondering how strong your employment brand might be, try the following exercise: Open a new tab in your Internet browser and bring up your company's website. Now, find the section of your site where a job candidate would research your business and apply for a job. How does your employment brand stack up against these three important success factors?

1. Can I easily submit an application?

Think about your digital marketing programs that focus on your market's consumer base. How much information do you ask of them when they submit a lead? Pretty much a name and email address, I'm guessing? You know the reason: The more fields on a leads form, the fewer leads you get.

It's no different with online job applications. The experience is everything. If you're asking applicants to give you their name, email address, and a resume, you're in good shape. If you're asking your applicants to completely re-create their resume on an online web form with dozens of fields—or, worse, forcing them to register a user account—you're making it much, much harder for them to apply than it needs to be.

Our research shows a nearly linear correlation between the number of fields on an online job application and the conversion rate of traffic to form submissions.

FIG 3.2—CONVERSION RATE FOR ONLINE JOB APPLICATIONS

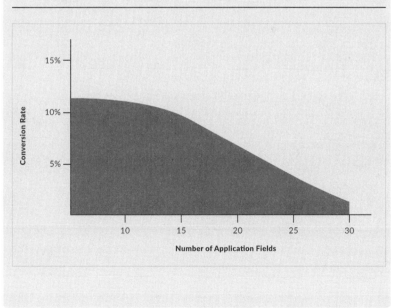

I strongly recommend keeping online job applications to eight fields or less. Like customer leads, the point is to generate interest and make contact; if you're running an effective interview process you'll have plenty of opportunity to vet candidates.

2. Does it work on a mobile phone?

You know that you're really missing the boat if your consumer site doesn't render well on a mobile device. Did you realize that these days, more than *60 percent* of all website traffic in the US and Canada originates from a mobile device?[6]

If a candidate can't open your careers page on a mobile phone, you're throwing away nearly two-thirds of your applicant traffic and drastically restricting your access to the strongest candidates in your local job market. Not to mention, you're wasting most of your investment in recruitment advertising.

Go ahead; try researching jobs at your company from your phone. How's the experience? Ask yourself, if I were looking for a job, does my company's careers page make this a good experience? If the answer is anything other than "yes," you've got work to do.

3. Does it tell a compelling story?

The market for top talent will always be hypercompetitive, and you no longer have the luxury of being undisciplined when it comes to attracting the best talent. Job seekers, especially the 50 percent of the workforce that's made up of Millennials, want to work for an employer that provides a great working environment and a defined career path.

---

6   Samuel Greengard, "Geomarketing: It's Where It's At Today," Internet Marketing Association, July 24, 2014, http://imanetwork.org/geomarketing-today.

A career site is more than a listing of open jobs—it needs to be exciting and reflect your company's history, culture, community involvement, and employee quality of life. Ask yourself: Does your career site explain the professional growth potential for a new employee? Does it tell the story of who you are and what you stand for? Does it give me a compelling reason to want to work for you?

The Schomp career site is an excellent example because they've built it so that it supports any mobile device, streamlines the application process, and masters the art of telling their own story. The Schomp Automotive site clearly shows potential applicants the reasons Schomp is an employer of choice. If I'm shopping for a job, Schomp presents a compelling case for why they deserve my time and attention.

It's time for you to treat your employment brand with the same level of rigor and quality control that you do with your customer brand. In these increasingly competitive and uncertain times, your success rests on your ability to hire and retain great people. Great people want to work for great companies; make sure that your employment brand meets today's standards.

fig 3.3—A Strong Employment Brand Requirements

 1. Easy Online Application

2. Mobile Friendly Interface

3. Compelling Company Narrative

Attracting Millennial Employees

Millennials are a group of technologically savvy and innovative young people. This generational cohort is often misunderstood by employers, who have assigned adjectives like "entitled" and "lazy" to describe how this group approaches work. While these characterizations are not accurate, Millennials do have different, evolving expectations of what it means to be an employee. They're also your future workforce. It's imperative that you attract them to your company, which means that it's high time you understand what motivates this generation. Here's what they want:

Consistent Training and a Career Path

Millennials want to learn and progress. A key way to show that you're invested in their future and to convince them to commit to your company's future is to provide training that will let them grow in their roles and progress in their careers.

Clear Expectations and Regular Reviews

The Millennial generation wants shorter-term gratification. Make sure they know exactly what you expect from them on any given task, and regularly let them know how they are progressing with regular check-ins and informal feedback. Once-a-year reviews with unclear goals will not keep them engaged or committed.

Reasonable Work–Life Balance

Whether this means promoting work–life integration, offering tools and opportunity for mobility and flexibility, or changing the way you staff your company's shifts, Millennials demand to have and enjoy their personal time outside of work.

Superior Company Culture

Engagement is essential to the success of your business. Millennials must feel connected with their organization to stay engaged with their work. You can create enthusiasm for your company by encouraging healthy relationships between your employees. You can also attract good workers by clearly defining your company's values and purpose. Once they are hired, a positive company culture will make employees think twice about finding a new job.

Creating Recruitment Processes with Retention in Mind

Retention is a crucial issue for many companies. After spending significant time and money to attract and hire employees, you probably want them to stick around, right? To recruit top talent, you must ensure that you have a consistent, clearly defined hiring process. This will reduce the risk of turnover and poor performance. A poorly defined recruiting process will damage the bottom line when a bad hire or open position results in lost or reduced sales. Consider the following:

- *Treat job candidates the same as you would treat potential customers.*

  The strategies that companies use to create loyal customers are strikingly similar to emerging strategies that build engaged and happy work teams. A recent report by Human Resources consulting firm Towers Watson revealed that companies that have adopted an integrated employee value proposition are five times more likely than the average company to report their employees are highly engaged and are twice as likely to achieve financial performance significantly above their peers.[7]

---

7   Towers Watson, "Global Talent Management and Rewards Study," *Workspan*, May 2013.

It's a safe bet that you're already treating your customer leads like the valuable asset that they are—you're training your teams to follow up quickly, to engage, and to deliver value in every interaction. Are you treating your job applicants in the same way?

As it is with your prospective customers, lack of responsiveness with job seekers is a sure-fire way to create a terrible first impression. If a highly talented job candidate doesn't sense that you care, they'll quickly seek out a more appealing employer. Millennials in particular expect instant gratification—if you're not quick to respond when they apply for your open job, you'll lose out.

- *Double-check the language in your job listings.*

You put substantial effort to make your product offerings appealing to customers, and jobs are no different. Your job listings may contain language that alienates your ideal candidates. Do your postings put your company in the best light? Do you provide information about career paths, benefits, and your culture? When you read your job listings, is it abundantly clear who you are and what your company stands for? Does it give the candidate a compelling reason to apply?

- *Attract a diverse pool of applicants.*

Multiple studies on the impact of diversity on business performance show that diverse workforces produce better financial results. In its 2015 report "Diversity Matters," management consulting firm McKinsey & Company examined proprietary data sets for 366 public companies across a range of industries in Canada, Latin America, the United Kingdom, and the United States.[8] McKinsey

---

8   Vivian Hunt, Dennis Layton, Sara Prince, "Diversity Matters," McKinsey and Company, February 2, 2015.

analyzed metrics such as financial results and the composition of top management and boards. The results speak for themselves:

- Companies in the top quartile for racial and ethnic diversity are 35 percent more likely to have financial returns above their respective national industry medians.

- Companies in the top quartile for gender diversity are 15 percent more likely to have financial returns above their respective national industry medians.

- Companies in the bottom quartile both for gender, ethnicity, and race are statistically less likely to achieve above-average financial returns.

- In the United States, for every 10 percent increase in racial and ethnic diversity on a company's senior-executive team, earnings before interest and taxes (EBIT) rise 0.8 percent.

The unequal performance of companies in the same industry and country implies that diversity is a competitive differentiator shifting market share toward more diverse companies.

Thoughtfully crafted job postings encourage a diverse pool of high-quality candidates to apply. The opposite is also true. For example, words that have overly masculine connotations that make your company sound like a boys-only club. Examples of these phrases used in recruiting sales professionals include descriptors such as "rock star," "sales ninja," "only assertive reps need apply," or "aggressive closers wanted." Using images of high-fiving Caucasian males on your company's careers page isn't helping, either.

Take time to craft descriptors for the position that will appeal to a diverse applicant pool. With respect to gender diversity, research shows that female candidates desire work environments that encourage collaboration, transparency, and have upper-level managers who are focused on developing their skills. The most effective method to encourage women to apply for open positions is to show them that your workforce is already diverse,[9] as evidenced in a study by Yale and the Albert Einstein College of Medicine about gender imbalances in male-dominated fields. You can showcase your diversity by having women present at job fairs and by employing company messaging that is consistent with your hiring goals.

• *Don't go with your gut; instead, employ a smart hiring system.*

Your emotional feeling about an employee based on a resume or quick phone call can be misleading. You need to have clearly spelled out, objective criteria for each job opening.

Without an understanding of Millennial workers and a game plan to hire and retain them, you will struggle with turnover and run out of top talent to hire. Implementing these steps to attract and retain Millennials will ensure the future success of your business.

Now that you understand employment branding and the concept of treating candidates as you treat your customers, let's talk about how to go about sourcing candidates for an open position.

Treating Recruitment like a Sales Process

Human Resources executives face a nearly impossible task. CEOs tell them to train the company's new employees, pay them accurately,

---

9   Albert Einstein College of Medicine, "Boost career of female scientists: make sure women help choose meeting speakers," EurekAlert, January 7, 2014, http://www.eurekalert.org/pub_releases/2014-01/aeco-bco010214.php.

make them happy and healthy, and rate their performance. At the same time, HR must adjudicate all disputes, retain the best people, manage employee retirement plans, and create a roadmap to staff the company for the next five years, too.

Here's a heartfelt "I get it" to my readers in the HR profession.

Human Resources is typically great at maintaining processes like benefits, payroll, and training, but recruiting is almost always a sore spot where it's a constant struggle to deliver on management's expectations. The root of this issue is that HR, as a general rule, oversees administrative functions. They maintain programs, processes, and keep things running. HR may be good at managing people, but recruiting, at its core, is a *sales* function. When you have an outward facing, go-get-'em operation like recruiting run by an administrative function like HR, you may be suboptimizing your results.

To see how similar recruiting is to sales, let's look at how recruiters do what they do. The recruiter first mines their databases for people who may be a good fit for their open position, just like sales and marketing teams mine a customer relationship management (CRM) system like Salesforce.com looking for leads. Recruiters then cold-call or email candidates with a job proposition, just like a salesperson calls on a prospect. In either case, it's work that requires one to check their ego at the door, because you get nine "nos" for every one "yes." Recruiters then pitch the company to a candidate, similar to how a salesperson has their first phone meeting with a prospect. If the candidate likes what they hear, they come in for another meeting. At the final stage, the recruiter makes an offer to their candidate, who either accepts or rejects it based on their other options.

How many HR staffers do you know who like to bang out a hundred cold calls a day? How many administrators have you worked with who enjoy the rough-and-tumble of convincing someone to change their incumbent choice and instead buy from your company? If you're going to run a world-class recruiting operation, you need to call it what it is—a sales team.

Would you, as the head of your company, put HR in the impossible position of running the sales operation? Of course not. Then why do you have your HR leader chasing down your managers—the ones with the open roles—and begging them to get involved? Why aren't the business managers the ones tasked with managing the selling of your company to new prospective employees?

Recruiting is a sales function. The companies that understand this will win the war for talent. Those that don't will overspend on recruiting and still come up short.

Where to Find Candidates

There are five primary channels you can use to find job applicants, each of which has varying degrees of speed, quality, and cost:

⊙	SPEED	how quickly will I get people?
✔	QUALITY	to what degree can I control candidate quality through this channel?
$	COST	how much will it cost me to hire someone through this channel?

Each of the following options for finding potential hires falls on a different point on the Recruiting Efficiency Index based on these three measures.

Recruiting Efficiency Index

I. Job Boards

Until recently, if you were an employer who wanted to get the word out that you were hiring, you posted an ad in your local paper. For decades, news-

papers earned billions of dollars a year from these ads. The Internet changed all that. The debut of Craigslist in 1995 was the moment when traditional print media, which counted on all those ad revenues to make their business model work, began its downturn. Started by a programmer named Craig Newmark as a way to share updates with his friends, Craigslist completely disrupted the classified ads market because it didn't charge to post ads for open jobs. Just as importantly, everything was now online and searchable. The job search market would never be the same.

Over time, other players like Careerbuilder, Monster, and Dice entered the market for online job postings. Sites like these provide essentially the same classified ad service that newspapers used to, with employers paying fees that range from $100 to $500 to post their job opening. I call this approach the *post and pray* method, and it works well when the supply of candidates exceeds the number of jobs available. If you pay $400 to advertise your job opening for a position that will likely have a lot of candidates such as a sales or retail job, the amount of potential candidate traffic you'll get in response should be worth the money you spend. On the other hand, if the job you are looking to fill has a limited supply of candidates—say you need to hire a nuclear physicist who speaks Mandarin and who has top secret government clearance—you might find that you don't get much return on your investment because those candidates don't exist *en masse*.

Many people in the hiring world have developed a love–hate relationship with job boards. When it works well, and you get a lot of potential candidates applying for your open job, you're happy. When it doesn't work and you don't get any candidates to apply, you feel like you wasted your money. Short of any viable alternative, most consider posting on these boards a necessary evil: something you just have to do.

Pay-Per-Click

One recent innovation that has grown in popularity is the use of pay-per-click job postings that work similarly to Google's AdWords program. In this model, you only pay the site posting your job opening when someone clicks on it. The upside of this approach is that you can control your budget more effectively than if you just pay a flat fee. If no one clicks on your ad, you don't have to pay anything. The downside is that if you get a ton of traffic to your ad, you might end up burning through your budget in just a day or two.

The pay-per-click approach is effective as long as you actively manage the bidding and budgeting process. You need to treat this process like your online marketing. You need to drive as many leads as you can into the top of your sales funnel and convert them into qualified candidates, just as you would with prospective customers. Making this process work is all about digging into the economics of the job boards so that you can calculate your cost per applicant (the total cost of your ad budget divided by the number of applicants you get). Job boards are most effective when your conversion rate is higher than its average, which means you have a lower cost per applicant.

This is where having a strong employment brand pays for itself. When you can drive more candidates to your career site without having to pay for those high-quality leads, you'll save money and wind up with better candidates. Our research shows that when a career site generates organic candidate traffic, the average cost per applicant is approximately $245. When a company uses a third-party source like a job board, the average cost is much higher at $1,700. You can truly realize a healthy return on investment with your employment brand.

Hireology conducted a case study for an automotive dealership with six different locations. We conducted an analysis of where different candidates for their open positions came from and which ones were eventually hired.

We found that although job boards generated plenty of candidate leads, the people who came directly to the company's career site were the majority of their new hires. In this case, 20 percent of the traffic yielded 80 percent of the company's new employees. Candidates who are drawn to you by your employment brand are more likely to be A- or B-level players and have a higher retention rate. Combining strong employment branding with a data-driven evaluation process is one of the best investments your business can make. A strong brand and predictive hiring process produces better results.

2. Social Media

Companies have learned the value of connecting with consumers using social media. Many companies have yet to realize that they can use these same social

media channels to broadcast their employment opportunities. Your customers—the people who love your brand—could become your next employees. Have you had the experience of working with a customer who loved your company so much they asked what it was like to work there? How about having one of your employees refer a customer to an open position because of how much they love the company?

Research shows that people who love a company's brand are more likely to trust that company as an employer. Using your existing social media infrastructure to inform your biggest fans about your open positions is a win-win. You can attract high-caliber candidates at virtually no extra cost.

However, if you don't already have an active social media following, trying to leverage social media for employment opportunities alone might prove distracting and unproductive. Be honest about where you stand. If you haven't already spent the time, money, and effort to develop these channels, you will be less likely to create the critical mass required to attract qualified candidates.

Let's talk about some of the prominent players in social media, some of the emerging platforms, and how you can use social media to attract your next great hire.

Twitter

Founded in 2006, Twitter has grown to more than three hundred million active users. Twitter allows you to post 140-character messages, called *tweets*, which are broadcast to anyone who is *following* you. Many brands now use Twitter to converse with their followers and update them on products and services. Why not use Twitter to let people who are engaged with your brand know about your job openings? You can send out a tweet letting people know about an open position and include a link to where they can apply on your career site. Twitter now also allows you to pay to promote your tweets—another way to advance your job openings.

Facebook

Famously founded by Mark Zuckerberg, Facebook is one of the largest and most influential technology companies worldwide. Although it was originally for college students, Facebook has since become an important platform for companies to connect and engage with their fans. This makes it an effective and cost-efficient platform for posting your open positions. You can now leverage Facebook's pay-per-click advertising program as a way to target a broader audience as well.

LinkedIn

Another hugely popular social media platform is LinkedIn. Founder Reid Hoffman's vision was to create a Facebook-like social network that would be dedicated to professionals and employment. Since its start in 2003, LinkedIn has grown into a great place to post jobs and send out alerts to your network. LinkedIn tends to perform much better for professional, white-collar jobs and not as well for skilled, technical, or hourly positions.

Other Emerging Channels

The social media landscape continues evolving as newer players like YouTube, Instagram, Pinterest, and Snapchat gain traction as a way for people and brands to connect. Although none of these channels was created specifically for promoting an employment brand or for posting jobs, they are effective ways for your company to connect to an audience of followers about what it's like to work at your business. These channels are extremely popular with the coveted eighteen- to thirty-four-year-old demographic, and marketers are willing to spend whatever it takes to connect with them. If you make that investment, why not leverage that same channel to let people know you are hiring, as well?

3. Search Firms

The recruiting industry makes an estimated $90 billion a year, for good reason. Recruiters—whether on your staff or through a third-party agency—make your life better by taking care of the sourcing, sorting, screening, and filtering of hundreds of resumes and boiling them down to the three to five finalists you need. They know who's available and what their needs are. The best recruiters act as human capital advisors for your firm, counseling you on issues like compensation, and some even develop a job profile on your behalf.

Recruiters aren't cheap; it's common for retained executive recruiters to charge as much as 40 percent of the new employee's total first year compensation as a fee. The majority of recruitment agencies work on a contingency basis, meaning that they only get paid when you make a new hire, and charge an average of 20–25 percent. So, for a $100,000 position you're looking at a fee of $20,000 to $30,000. Ouch.

The proliferation of job boards and the advent of social networks have made the sourcing stage of the recruiting process much easier. Still, there are recruiters that specialize in this new throughput model of recruiting. These recruiters take care of sourcing and screening candidates and then let you take over the hiring process from the interview stage forward. When you're ready to begin searching for candidates, it behooves you to check out the recruiting service options that are out there—and there are hundreds of options. For companies that hire at high volumes each month, it may be more efficient to outsource all or part of your recruiting process. The vendors in this level of recruiting are known as recruitment process outsourcing (RPO) firms.

Recruiters can greatly accelerate your search process, regardless of your company's size and need. Their access to tools and resources that you simply don't have time to deal with makes them a valuable partner to have. However, this option is a lot less scalable than the DIY model due to the high cost-per-hire.

Debunking the Myth of Active versus Passive Candidates

The recruitment industry buckets job seekers into two main groups: active candidates and passive candidates. *Active candidates* are defined as people who are actively looking for a job or have their resume posted on a job board. *Passive candidates* are defined as people who are not actively looking for a job and who don't have their resumes on a job board but would consider a new position if it were presented to them.

My colleagues in the recruitment and assessment industry love to talk to their clients about the differences between active and passive candidates. The prevailing sentiment among professional recruiters is that active candidates are lower quality and that passive candidates are higher quality. This belief is based entirely on the assumption that people who are looking for work can't possibly be as good as people who are happily employed. Active candidates, these recruiters say, post their jobs on job boards because they can't hack it where they're currently working. Passive candidates, the talking points read, are better because you have to pry them out of their current job.

I disagree.

Whether or not a candidate is or isn't looking for work doesn't automatically make them a good fit or a bad fit for your open position. Regardless of whether a recruiter calls them active or passive, these candidates still must be vetted accordingly. Making broad assumptions about the quality and disposition of candidates will cause you to overlook the lowest cost and highest payoff recruiting tools out there. Maintain the active versus passive bias and you'll be handicapping your company's recruiting efforts for years to come.

Based on the latest statistics, the average job tenure for an early to midcareer employee is just under three years. That is to say, a person will keep the same job for about three years before deciding to look for work. This creates a high volume of people actively looking for work at any given time—around thirty million people, according to some estimates. Consider that people in their twenties and thirties tend to have a smaller professional network of decision makers at businesses than do people in their forties and fifties. This reality pushes younger workers online to find job opportunities, because they have no professional network to tap. The expansion and adoption of Internet job boards like LinkedIn, Careerbuilder, and even Craigslist have made it easier for employees and recruiters to connect online. Together these factors mean that there is a robust online talent market filled with millions of high-quality resources, and it is growing every year.

The fact that the recruitment industry is still even talking about active versus passive candidates is a worrisome statement about the state of the traditional recruitment business model. For the past fifty years, headhunters dominated the landscape because they had built up massive, Rolodex-based databases of candidates. These databases were created with blood, sweat, tears, and a lot of cold calling. These Rolodexes were the intellectual property of the recruitment business, and firms charged a pretty penny for access.

Then, the Internet and online job boards ruined the Rolodex party. Now, a tech-savvy recruiter can use tools like LinkedIn and replicate a headhunter's database in approximately eight seconds. The proliferation of these technologies and high-volume candidate traffic on job boards has spawned an entirely new low-cost recruitment business with models like recruitment process outsourcing (RPO) and offshore sourcing.

Although finding senior-level executives like CEOs, CFOs, and some VPs largely remains a Rolodex recruiting game, as Internet savvy Gen X and Millennial superstars move up the corporate ladder, their comfort with and use of job boards and social networking sites will make it easier for recruiters to find them. This change should have the large corporate headhunting firms worried. Most retained search providers constantly downplay the viability of active candidates by playing the low-quality card to the company's disadvantage. If these recruiters don't have a Rolodex to sell, what do they have of value?

There's no substantive difference between active and passive candidates. Instead, there are merely candidates who are a fit for your role based on their career experience and those who are not.

Tell your recruiter that you don't care where your candidates come from. Just make sure they give you good ones.

How should you go about hiring a recruiter?

When you're considering hiring a third-party recruiter, there is a multitude of options. These recruiters run the range from a bare bones service with a low price to a full-service executive search that can cost a small fortune. The good news about recruiting services for consumers is that the prices are declining for most of these services and will continue to decline for the foreseeable future. Thanks, Internet!

Let's take a look at the third-party recruiting options available to entrepreneurs and business managers:

Executive and Retained Search Firms

Executive search firms are the granddaddy of the recruitment model and specialize in finding high-end professional talent. The

SPEED
QUALITY
COST

largest executive search firms, such as Heidrick & Struggles and Korn Ferry, spend the majority of their time recruiting C-level executives and board members for publicly traded companies. These executive search firms are comprised of partners who have deep domain expertise in their industry niche (logistics, energy, banking, etc.) and who know every executive in the industry by name. They should be able to tell you this level of detail, because they charge a king's ransom for their services.

These firms charge what's called a *retainer*, an up-front, nonrefundable recruiting fee. The retainer is typically 30–40 percent of a candidate's first year total compensation and is payable in one-third increments. For example: A $300,000-a-year CEO would represent a fee of $100,000 and up, depending on whether or not the client has negotiated a fee cap.

Pro: Executive search firms work until the job is filled, and the best executive recruiters have a lock on the best talent in any given industry.

Con: The price tag is out of reach for most small and midsized businesses. When was the last time you spent $100,000 to find someone?

Contingency Search Firms

The contingent search model is the most widely used recruitment business model and the one that you are probably familiar with. Contingent

SPEED
QUALITY
COST

search firms, companies such as Robert Half and MRINetwork, charge a fee that's contingent on you hiring a candidate whom they've sent to you for consideration. Fees for contingent search firms typically fall in the range of 20–30 percent of the first year's salary, and fees have been steadily falling for the past ten years.

Pro: You only pay contingency search firms a fee if you make a hire.

Con: There are many, many cons. First, the expansive reach of the Internet has made it easier to access information. This increased access means that you're overpaying contingency search firms for information that you could hire someone to find for a lot less. Second, when you negotiate a reduced fee with a contingent search firm, you are increasing the likelihood that they're sending you their B-level candidates. How is this possible? Well, think about it for a second. If you're Joe Search Firm Owner and you have a relationship with a superstar candidate who you know is in high demand, and you know that you only get paid if someone hires *your* candidate—are you going to send the superstar candidate to the company that's paying you a 30 percent fee or the company that's paying you a 20 percent fee? The company paying the higher fee will get the better candidates. If you're sitting there feeling good about sticking it to your search firm with a low-fee arrangement, understand that you're setting yourself up to get the less-desirable candidates. This harsh reality exacerbates your problem by forcing you to waste your time with bench players.

Recruitment Process Outsourcing Firms (RPOs)

The recruitment process outsourcing model (RPO) has been around for about ten years. The RPO model is when a vendor seeks to leverage infrastructure costs across a variety

SPEED

QUALITY

COST $ $ $

of clients to deliver lower per-hire costs. Most RPO vendors charge a monthly administration cost and a per-hire fee for every person successfully placed.

Pro: Most of your recruitment costs are variable, and you can hold a vendor's feet to the fire with a service agreement.

Con: Most RPOs are just going to post your job to the same places you could post it yourself. Additionally, RPOs only do the initial screening. You're probably paying more per candidate than you need to pay.

Offshore Sourcing Firms

Offshore recruiting firms provide a trade-off between price and quality. You can hire an offshore recruiting firm for less than $2,000 a month, but you will get mostly raw, unscreened resumes that have been gleaned from major job boards. If you're not doing any recruiting on your own, offshore sourcing firms may at least help you to increase candidate volume. But if you're already subscribing to a few job boards, then these firms are likely more hassle than they're worth. I anticipate that these firms will get much, much better as they gain more experience.

SPEED	🕐 🕐 🕐 🕐
QUALITY	✔ ✔
COST	$ $

Pro: You get huge leverage for your money and lots of candidates.

Con: The resumes you receive are mostly scraped from job boards. The quality and fit of the candidates are typically much lower than the other options discussed here. Additionally, the time zone differences between your company and the firm can be tough to manage, as well as any language differences or communication gaps.

Contract Recruiters

If all else fails, you can hire a full-time recruiter on a contract basis to help you through a hiring spike. These recruiters are 1099 or corp-to-corp resources who

SPEED

QUALITY

COST $ $ $ $

have been working in the industry for several years, often in multiple industries. Look to pay anywhere from $40–$70 per hour for a solid contract recruiter.

Pro: Contract recruiters come to your company, so you have maximum flexibility. They do what you ask them to do. If they have local experience, they likely have candidate networks established and are experienced with a number of different job types.

Con: Contract recruiters can be expensive, and at the end of the day they're still only one person.

4. Staffing Companies

Another option you can leverage for bringing on candidates is a staffing agency. A staffing agency does the initial sourcing and screening of candidates. The employees that they send to you are employees on *their* payroll, not yours. When you place a request with a staffing agency, they will presumably send you prescreened and qualified candidates that you put to work on a kind of try-before-you-buy basis. Although you are paying the staffing agency a fee, you get to evaluate the person's skills, personality, and cultural fit. If you like what you see, you can then increase the stakes by hiring that person on full time. If things don't work out, you can just call up the staffing agency and ask for them to send you a replacement.

Pro: Staffing agencies are low risk to you, because you can let hires go at any time and let the staffing company worry about the paperwork.

Con: These agencies are expensive and the candidate quality varies. Contingency labor also comes with an increasing amount of co-employment liability risks. If you don't know what that means, call your attorney.

5. Referral Programs

Referrals are powerful. Not only are referrals the lowest cost source for great job candidates, they are also the way you find the candidates with the

highest probability of succeeding. Research conducted by the consulting firm Deloitte found that employees who were hired via referrals stayed in their new jobs longer than employees who were hired via job boards or career sites.[10]

You can simply and effectively kick off a referral program by printing out a stack of cards that showcase your company's logo, your hiring manager's name, and the URL to your career site. Hand out these cards to all of your managers and encourage them to give the cards to anyone who impresses them or who might address a need inside your organization. Your managers can easily let a person know they would be a perfect fit for the organization and that they should apply for a job on your career website. The manager can then promise to look out for the application, flag the materials, and push the candidate through the hiring process. Using this process lets the

---

10   Katherine Jones, PhD, & Kim Lamoureux, *Creating an Employee Referral Program: Guideline for Getting Started*, Bersin by Deloitte, December 2013.

candidate know they have someone pulling for them and encourages them to apply.

You never know when you will run into people who will make great candidates for your open positions, and your managers need to be armed with a way to connect with potential employees in a friendly and encouraging manner. It doesn't matter if you meet them at a car rental counter or if you sit next to them on a flight, if you have a quick elevator pitch and a card at the ready, you are more likely to get that person to apply for a job. A CEO client of ours once told me a great story about how, while working late one night, he pulled in to the drive-through of a Taco Bell to get a bite to eat. Then, he struck up a great conversation with the employee working at the window. Even though it was two a.m., the woman helping him was extremely cheerful and helpful. The CEO was so impressed that after he got his food, he parked his car and walked up to the window to offer the woman a job at his company. You never know when you're going to meet a potential great hire. You need to be ready to pounce on those opportunities when they pop up.

Building Employee Referral Programs

An employee referral program is a formal program that rewards employees who refer candidates who end up working for your organization. Most of these programs pay employees a cash bonus if the person they refer is hired and stays with the organization somewhere between six and twelve months.

Not all managers like programs that work this way; they loathe the idea of paying their employees for something as simple as a referral. But these feelings are mistaken. Calculate how much you are spending on everything from job boards and social media to recruiters and staffing firms. Then divide that figure by the number of hires you make.

That's your cost-per-hire. On average, most companies spend between $2,000 and $3,000 to recruit a new hire.

Wouldn't it make sense to pay an employee $1,000 if they refer a candidate to the organization who is a perfect fit? You get a great hire at about half the cost. You could even structure the bonus so that you pay it out incrementally based on how long the new hire stays with the organization. Maybe you pay 25 percent after six months, for example, and pay the remainder of the bonus after a year. If the new hire doesn't work out, then you don't have to pay. An employee referral program creates incentives for your best employees to refer other good people to your business. Great employees like to work with other great people, so create ways to pay them for bringing those people in. You will make great hires at half the cost. With the help of an effective employee referral program, you come out ahead.

Case Study: Experience Isn't Everything When It Comes to Hiring

The labor market will go through a talent crunch in the coming decades, and organizations might not have the luxury of hiring qualified candidates who come with experience. You may need to rethink how and where you look for candidates who can grow into the roles you need to fill.

"Look beyond the big-name colleges and universities that many potential A-players can't afford to attend anymore," says Jeff Ellman, a serial entrepreneur who has started businesses in several industries, including the recruiting business.

He says that employers need to expand their talent searches when they look for young candidates because a good employee can come from anywhere. Employers need to be constantly on the lookout for new talent.

"Recruiting is not a light switch you can throw on," Ellman says. "Great companies are always looking for great talent."

Based on his years of experience, Ellman likes to say that he's interviewed more people than Oprah, Letterman, and Leno combined.

"I've seen a lot of resumes over the years," says Ellman. Ellman founded a company called Humatal in 1999 that recruited students on college campuses. Shortly after, Ellman was hired by other companies to pick out the best and brightest among the college ranks, despite many of those students not having any work experience.

He learned to prioritize other aspects over experience whenever he interviewed a potential hire.

"I always look for things I can't teach like attitude, work ethic, communication skills, and personality," says Ellman.

He also watches a candidate's nonverbal body language for cues, along with other things like whether they might be wearing too much cologne and what time they show up for their interview.

"It was amazing how many times candidates would walk in to an interview with a stamp still on their hands from hitting the bars the night before," he says.

Although a college student's resume might not have a lot of work experience listed, Ellman looks for pattern recognition in a candidate's experience, especially when assessing a candidate's leadership potential. If someone was voted president of their class and was captain of the basketball team, for example, or was involved in leading the student body or a sorority in college, "then there was a high likelihood that those same leadership patterns would carry through to their career," says Ellman.

Ellman also prioritizes writing ability during his screening process. Writing is essential in the working world; employees can craft everything from emails to blog posts.

"I have made the mistake of hiring people who appeared good on paper," he says, "but then their writing skills are so horrible they couldn't interact with customers."

Additionally, Ellman screens candidates on how coachable they may be. To do that, he might ask a sales candidate to perform a role-playing exercise where they would try and sell a fictional product or service. Ellman would then give the candidate feedback about how they could have done it better and have them run through the exercise again. By doing this, he can see if they took his advice or not.

Ellman also wants to know that a candidate has done some research on the job and the company. What really impresses him, though, is when a candidate asks for the job at the end of the interview.

"Most people never close the interview," he says. "They don't say something like, 'Based on what I learned today, I can see this as a place I want to work.' When someone says they want the job, that's a tie-breaker for me. I go with the person who wanted it more and communicated it better."

• • •

CHAPTER SUMMARY

Once you have identified exactly what roles you need to fill and the kind of people you want to fill them, it's time to get the word out to potential candidates. Thinking of your recruiting efforts like you would approach a sales process is essential. Approaching hiring in this way requires a significant investment in time, money, and resources to be effective.

You can begin this transformation by making sure you are investing in the strength of your employment brand. Ensure your company has a modern and functioning career page on your website that makes it easy for candidates to learn about the company and apply to open positions. When attracting Millennials to your brand, be sure you are clear about the values your organization has and how your employees can expect to grow their career with you.

When it comes to finding great people, you can also cast a wider net by using third-party resources like job boards, social media networks, and recruiters. Close management and understanding your per-hire cost on these platforms is key to making these investments pay off. For the best return on your recruiting investments, create a referral program that makes it easy for your hiring managers and employees to encourage great people they know to apply for your open positions.

SELF-ANALYSIS

Ask yourself the following questions:

- Who is in charge of your hiring process? Do they get the same attention and resources as your sales team?

- What is the experience like when someone applies for a job at your company? Go online to your career site and see.

- How can you begin to leverage the investments you have made in social media channels to attract great employees?

KEY TAKEAWAYS

1   Make hiring as important to your organization as sales; you'll be more profitable as a result.

2   Invest in your employment brand and learn to share the promise of what it's like to work in your organization to attract better candidates, including Millennials.

3   Understand what you currently spend on every hire to better manage the recruiting and hiring process and to get more bang for your buck.

4   Leverage your social media channels to connect with your biggest fans—fans can become great employees.

5   Start a referral program. You never know where your next great hire will come from.

SELECT THE RIGHT PERSON

Chapter Four

BUILD A CANDIDATE SCORECARD

When I was in high school, my family took a Saturday trip to Arlington Park, a horse racing track and well-known fixture of suburban Chicago. It was a sweltering summer afternoon in the Midwest, with temperatures hovering just above 90 degrees. The enormous grandstand was packed with a mishmash of patrons. There were families with kids and grizzled racetrack veterans who walked around with entire newspapers rolled up and shoved in their pants pockets.

I was absolutely fascinated. It was my first experience in a betting establishment. I couldn't stop staring at the racetrack vets with their sharpened pencils and crib sheets. They would pore over numbers in their newspapers, scouring the pages for that secret bit of information that would give them the edge over the poor saps around them. These guys were *into* this stuff.

Then, there was my father. He was there for the fun of it and was just having a good time with Mom and us kids. I watched him fill out his betting card seemingly randomly. I decided that Dad didn't give a rat's hind end about horse wagering.

"Dad," I asked, around the fourth race of the day, "how do you decide which horse you're going to pick?"

"Easy," he replied, a smirk in the corner of his mouth, "I pick the horse that poops."

It was the first time in my life that I had heard that old cliché about betting on horses and dogs, and I recall thinking it was the funniest thing I had ever heard. Dad's system is something I now jokingly refer to as the *Arlington Method*, a system that novices use as a guidepost when they have no clue on how to select a winning horse. Just like with picking winning horses, the Arlington Method has no place when it comes to picking new hires.

Rating Candidates—Don't Wing It!

Deciding to hire an employee without a data-based system for vetting them is akin to trying to pick a horse based on little more than a gut feeling. There are more accurate ways to make a bet and figure out which candidate will perform the best.

To move beyond rating candidates using random pieces of information, we can build a *Candidate Scorecard*. Based on the job profile that we created in chapter two, a candidate scorecard rates applicants based on predefined competencies that you've determined are crucial to a new employee's success in the role. This method ensures that you rate all candidates based on the same criteria and make a decision that's based on data, not just gut feelings or a haphazard Arlington Method.

A candidate scorecard serves as your judging guide throughout the recruiting life cycle. In addition to serving as a central repository for your notes on an applicant's abilities, the candidate scorecard provides you with a common platform for objectively scoring all candidates for a particular position.

As entrepreneurs and managers, most of us believe that we have an above average ability to size up a person in a short amount of time.

We trust our gut feelings and rely on first impressions. It's no wonder that we operate this way, because our insane workloads often demand we take action instead of allowing us time to analyze data. But when selecting a candidate for an open position, winging it can lead to a potentially crippling poor hire and a lot of lost money.

There's a growing body of research that suggests gut decisions and first impressions carry with them the risk of substantial bias when it comes to hiring and candidate screening. In *Blink,* best-selling author Malcolm Gladwell's incredible book on rapid cognition (first impressions), the author cites meta-research produced from four large research studies showing that "when corrected for variables like age and gender and weight, an inch of height is worth $789 a year in salary." In conclusion, Gladwell posits, "Despite believing that we make rational decisions based on objective criteria, pre-existing biases toward traits like height, weight, and hair length have a huge influence on our assessment of others."[11]

Winging it, or hiring based on your gut feelings, is too risky to continue doing. Choosing a candidate based on arbitrary factors and first impressions can lead to bad hires that have far-reaching, costly, and negative consequences for your business. Repeat after me, "I, [state your name], promise to start using candidate scorecards to drive my hiring decisions."

Introducing Competency-Based Hiring

After poor hires cost my first company over a million dollars in wasted salaries and lost customers over the course of two years, adopting a

---

11   Malcom Gladwell, *Blink: The Power of Thinking Without Thinking* (New York: Little, Brown and Company, 2005).

competency-based approach to hiring and managing staff helped to put my business on sure footing. Competency-based hiring is for real.

What the Heck Is a Competency?

A competency is a specific set of skills, knowledge, qualifications, and capacities that a potential employee should have in order to perform the duties and responsibilities their manager assigns them.

In the Hireology Intelligent Hiring Platform, there are sixty-seven competencies that we use to evaluate the potential fit of a prospective employee. Using the data we've compiled from millions of applicants and hundreds of thousands of hires, we were able to create a data-driven framework for sorting through a person's experience to determine whether or not they have a likelihood of success in their potential role.

The system breaks down these competencies into three distinct groups: Performance Results, Performance Factors, and Interpersonal Skills.

Performance Results

Performance Results are competencies that describe whether a person has the ability to produce a high volume of quality work and achieve predetermined results. These competencies include the following:

Quality of Work

Does this person produce great output or results by doing the following? Do they, for example:

- Complete high-quality work with thoroughness and accuracy to achieve results?

- Follow standards and procedures thoroughly?

- Keep complete records?
- Pay adequate attention to detail?

Quantity of Work

Can this person get enough of the right things done? Do they, for example:

- Complete assignments by or before the deadline?
- Produce sufficient work in a limited amount of time?
- Maintain control of their work regardless of environmental pressures?
- Manage priorities?
- Accept new responsibilities, projects, and tasks?

When we evaluate candidates, it's the Performance Results that are weighted most heavily. These two competencies are crucial to success in *every* role that you'll define. The rest of the competencies provide specificity around job performance and are totally irrelevant if a person's work history falls short here. If a potential employee demonstrates a track record of low-quality output or substandard volume, what's the point of going any further? Will it matter that they have amazing interpersonal skills if they have no ability to get results?

Performance Factors

Performance Factors are our second major competency category. Performance Factors enable hiring managers to dive deep into a person's job history to understand *what* they do and *how* they do it.

Job Knowledge and Technical Application

What job and industry-specific skills does this person possess? Are they able to apply this knowledge to a successful outcome? Do they:

- Apply technical and professional skills to job requirements?
- Keep job knowledge and technical skills current?
- Use past experience to solve problems?
- Apply company and industry information?

Organization and Planning

Can they:

- Set priorities to optimize how they use their time?
- Engage in short- and long-term planning?
- Propose milestones that adequately measure progress?
- Adhere to schedules and plans?

Analytical and Problem Solving

Does this person:

- Understand and define problems clearly?
- Formulate realistic solutions?
- Participate actively in group problem solving?
- Anticipate and prevent problems?

Judgment and Decision Making

Does this person:

- Consider relevant alternatives before making decisions?
- Show timeliness and conviction in making good decisions?

Self-Improvement and Initiative

Do they:

- Respond with constructive activities after a manager's feedback?
- Participate in professional societies?
- Keep current with emerging knowledge and trends in their field?
- Accomplish tasks resourcefully?

Innovation and Creativity

Does this person:

- Generate workable ideas, concepts, and techniques?
- Attempt new approaches willingly?
- Simplify or improve procedures, techniques, and processes?

Interpersonal Skills

Interpersonal Skills are competencies that are crucial to a person's ability to work and interact with others, in addition to their ability to manage staff.

Communication

Can this person:

- Articulate ideas in a clear, concise, and appropriately assertive manner?

- Produce readable, concise, and articulate written documents?

- Write without misspellings and grammatical errors?

- Provide professional service to both internal and external clients?

Teamwork

Will this person:

- Assist others?

- Participate effectively and offer ideas in work teams?

- Listen and respond to others' suggestions or ideas?

- Prevent and resolve conflicts?

- Manage the team when needed, regardless of their job title?

Supervision

As a manager of others, can they:

- Execute directions and plans from their manager?

- Accept constructive criticism and feedback?

- Keep their manager involved and informed on a timely basis?

Now, let's talk about how we score these competencies.

Scoring Core Competencies

Remember grade school? (Oh, the days of eating paste and playing dodgeball.) Unless you were homeschooled, it's likely that your teachers used the A–F system to grade academic performance.

The top grade is an A, the best evaluation you can hope to earn, the goal. Didn't we all want to be a straight-A student?

When we were young, we might not have realized that out of all of the grades in this system, there is only *one* classification that signifies meeting the requirements of the class—A. Every other grade, from B through F, communicates varying degrees of substandard performance. Getting a B tells you that you weren't quite good enough, and an F tells you that you missed the mark by a mile. Every grade but A communicates varying degrees of missed expectations.

We grow up learning that there's one classification for meeting expectations (A) and four classifications for failing to meet expectations (B, C, D, and F).

A New Approach to Measuring Performance

Most business managers dread performance evaluations, because they believe the evaluations are arbitrary. Performance evaluations can be arbitrary because managers rarely use any objective criteria like numbers or metrics to tell us whether or not someone has performed to expectations. Research shows that most employees aren't aware of their managers' expectations of their performance.[12] If you've ever had the task of conducting performance reviews, you've probably worked on an excellent-good-fair-poor scale, not unlike the A–F system used

---

12   Marco Nink, "Many Employees Don't Know What's Expected of Them at Work," Gallup.com, October 13, 2015, http://www.gallup.com/businessjournal/186164/employees-don-know-expected-work.aspx.

in school. The majority of your reviews were probably goods and excellents. But how do you effectively go about evaluating someone's performance before they have even started working for you, during the interview process?

Allow me to offer a few thoughts on performance. As a business owner or manager, do you accept performance that's anything less than getting the job done? Are you okay with a missed deadline here and there? With an employee who provides great customer service *most* of the time? Or with someone who has marginal communication skills? Of course not! You demand excellence every day (damn right!). Why should I, as a manager, feel compelled to rate an employee at the top of the scale for doing the job that I am paying them to do? Why is simply meeting expectations deserving of an excellent rating? Isn't that what we pay someone to do, meet our expectations?

Why, then, do we constrain our thinking with a performance management scale that rewards getting the job done with an A? What's there to shoot for above that? What would happen if you had a system that made fulfilling the requirements of the job fall in the middle of the scale at a C and gave your staff an opportunity to exceed your standard expectations?

When we discuss performance evaluations when we're hiring a new employee, it's our job as the hiring manager to evaluate the candidate's job performance over their *entire career*. And as I've shown, doing that using existing methods makes performance evaluations little more than subjective exercises.

One of the principal issues that drove me to build this framework was how frustrated I was with how the rest of the business world seems to assume that getting an A is the pinnacle of performance, not the standard. I don't buy a mentality that believes that getting a B or C is acceptable. So, I created a scoring system that placed performing to expectations smack in the middle of the scale. I wanted to create a system based on a performance management philosophy that posits anything less than an A is unacceptable and disqualifies a person from employment with your company *at any level*. The system that I'm advocating requires A-level performance in each competency as a *prerequisite* of employment. Promotion and advancement are only possible when you *exceed* expected performance.

Before we move forward, let's spend a moment covering experience levels as they relate to evaluating the level at which someone can or should display certain capabilities. You wouldn't expect a $30,000-per-year entry-level sales hire to exhibit the same level of competency as a $275,000 C-level executive, right? My preferred way to look at this issue is similar to the perspective of recruitment consultant Geoff Smart, who describes an A-player as "someone who is in the top 10 percent of performance for their current level of compensation."

As that entry-level sales hire moves up the compensation ladder, the level of competency required to stay in the top 10 percent range rises. An A-player at $50,000 who gets promoted into a $75,000-per-year job will find themselves in much tougher competition to be in the top 10 percent at that new salary range. An employee who continues to rise to the top 10 percent of all performers as you promote them over the years is someone you fight to keep at all costs. As you read through the next section, keep this principle in mind.

The Five-Point Performance Scale

I recommend using a five-point scale for scoring performance and aptitude. Getting a 3 in this system is equivalent to the academic grade of A. Again, getting a 3 is equal to getting an A. Be there mentally before continuing. Ready?

5: Exceptional

A rating of 5 indicates performance two levels above the expected performance level. This person:

- Consistently exhibits *all* aspects of the competency in an exceptional manner.
- Significantly *exceeds* expectations on all objectives provided.
- *Always* achieves exceptional results well beyond those expected of someone at their salary grade or level.

Note: usage of this rating is highly limited (less than 5 percent).

4: Exceeds

A rating of 4 indicates performance one level above the expected performance level. This person:

- Consistently exceeds the normal expectations for the competency.
- Exceeds expectations on all objectives provided.
- Achieves results above and beyond those expected of someone at their salary grade or level.

3: Meets

A rating of 3 indicates performance that is expected of someone at their salary grade or level. This person:

- Consistently meets all expectations of the competency in a fully capable manner.
- Achieves results that are expected of someone at their salary grade or level, including meeting goals and objectives.

2: Marginal

A rating of 2 indicates performance that does not consis
expectations. This person:

- Performs many aspects of the competency in a capable manner.

- Meets *some* goals and objectives, but requires improvement to perform at the level that is expected of someone at their salary grade
or level.

- May require more supervision than expected to meet guidelines
for the competency.

- Could be the performance level of those *new* to a position.

1: Unsatisfactory

A rating of 1 indicates unacceptable performance and suggests a lack
of willingness or ability to perform to the level of expectation for the
competency. This person:

- Requires excessive supervision.

- Needs separation or reassignment unless performance improves
significantly.

What you'll find is that 70 percent of your employees will be solid
3s on most competencies. That's fantastic; it means that your employees are getting the job done. Some 10 percent of them will be 4s (and,
occasionally, 5s). These are your top performers, and they're the ones
you're grooming for that next level. About 20 percent of them will fall
into the less-than-3 range.

The implications are straightforward: The employees who scored
1s or 2s are either up or out; they must better their work or face

leaving the company. People that exhibit 3s are the lifeblood of your business. The people that exhibit 4 and 5 behavior are the ones you throw your heart and soul (and money) into training and retaining. They get the perks, promotions, and recognition. In short, you build your company around them.

Now that we know how to score candidates, let's begin the process of dissecting the information from the candidate resumes and initial phone screens.

Case Study: Hire for Attitude over Experience

When Tracy McCarthy joined SAVO Group—a high-growth, business-to-business software company in Chicago—as its executive vice president of human resources, she faced an immediate challenge. How do you recruit top tech talent in a competitive market? Until McCarthy was hired on, the company's hiring philosophy was to overpay for experienced people relative to their competitors, thus luring them away from other companies competing for the same scarce talent.

"The thinking was that the company didn't have time to grow talent so they needed to go out and get it," says McCarthy, who estimates that she has hired some 4,000 people over her career working for large companies like Target.

Eventually, prioritizing experience over cultural fit and attitude cost SAVO. Not only did paying top dollar for workers who didn't truly embrace the company's mission and values have an up-front price, it harmed the company in other ways. Younger and hungrier employees started to leave the company to pursue other opportunities because there was no clear career path inside the business.

"People at other companies were telling us that they loved hiring our people because they were so well trained," says McCarthy. "That's when we realized we couldn't keep spinning off talented people who didn't have room to grow. That wasn't scalable for us."

As a result, the company, which has 150 employees, was forced to do some restructuring by letting some staff members go. Although that was a necessary and positive move for the company, those employees who were let go did mar its employment brand to some degree on job board sites.

McCarthy's next challenge was to rethink SAVO's hiring philosophy and shift it to focusing on growing and developing the talent they had in-house. They also began hiring for potential and attitude, not just experience.

"Our priority became to find ways to attract the right folks who would work well in our culture," says McCarthy.

To help identify which candidates she should be targeting, McCarthy and her team went through an exercise where they looked at the key attributes that their star employees displayed. When they culled through all the data, those attributes boiled down to a passion for getting things done with limited resources and an ability to deal with constant change.

"We needed people who could be flexible and adaptable," says McCarthy. "We recognized that if someone wanted a nine a.m. to five p.m. job, they probably wouldn't be the right fit for us."

McCarthy also began a program that would train employees, not just managers, to be part of the teams that interview potential candidates to help assess if a candidate would be a match with what the team was looking for.

"We don't like to use the term 'fit' because we want people to come in and contribute to and enhance what we have today," she says. "We don't want to hire 'yes people.' We want people who will challenge us and to help us think more creatively."

McCarthy says the changes she and her team have put in place have started to pay dividends. Not only has the caliber of the people that have been recently hired been off the charts, the company's reputation and brand in the marketplace has begun a serious upward trend that will continue to deliver returns in the future.

• • •

CHAPTER SUMMARY

The hiring process is often too subjective. Many people in charge of hiring pride themselves on their ability to make great hiring decisions based on their gut, or because they find something to like in a candidate. But these gut decisions are like flipping a coin.

To hire great people, you need to embrace an approach to hiring that incorporates competency-based hiring, which gives you objective and measurable ways to evaluate candidates. You need to come up with an objective game plan about what you want to measure and how you plan to measure it, before you schedule any interviews.

SELF-ANALYSIS

Ask yourself the following questions:

- How do you make your hiring decisions? Is there a process?
- Are you interested in eliminating subjective and potentially biased measures in your hiring process?
- How do you evaluate a job candidate's prior performance?

KEY TAKEAWAYS

1 Move beyond gut decisions and relying on chance in hiring your people; it's time to build a scorecard.

2 Establish a concrete list of competencies a new job will require and an objective way to score those traits. This will increase your odds of making a great hire.

3 Define what an A-player looks like in your business; it will help them become easier to recognize when they walk in the door.

Chapter Five

NARROW THE RESULTS

Given the talent shortages hitting many industries, it's easy to see why hiring managers want to believe everything that they read about Joe or Jane Superstar. Resumes are nothing more than marketing documents designed to tell employers what they want to hear and get the candidate an interview. *People lie on their resumes.*

About half of the interviews that I've conducted have resulted in finding a false truth or misstatement on a candidate's resume. Most of these misrepresentations are seemingly benign, like a slight overstatement of sales production or describing a job as having a bit more management responsibility than it really did. A few of these lies are downright egregious, such as a candidate lying about a college degree or hiding the fact that they were fired for theft. No matter the degree to which their claims are untrue, you don't want a person who misrepresents themselves or their employment history on your payroll.

Most of these falsehoods can be caught in the first stage of the assessment process: the resume review.

Identifying the Resume Red Flags

It's important to learn how to recognize the five common resume red flags. Identifying these potential issues will enable you to target your questioning and prevent you from wasting your time and money chasing after bad apples.

Red Flag I: Gaps in Employment

Everyone knows that employment gaps can signal a potential problem with an applicant, yet I am constantly reminding our customers that they need to dig, dig, and dig into employment gaps until they are satisfied that they're getting a straight answer. Gaps in employment on a resume can mean three things:

1. The person was either laid off or fired

Being laid off doesn't mean that someone is a bad employee (far from it), nor does being fired indicate malfeasance. These things *do*, however, mean that a candidate has some explaining to do. How big was the layoff? How many rounds of layoffs were there? In what round were they let go? Being the first one to go means the applicant is not as strong as someone who was kept on until the last possible moment through four rounds of layoffs. If they were fired . . . why? Was the candidate fired for a disagreement with their manager, or did they violate a company policy? Did they break the law?

2. The person quit without another job lined up

It always surprises me how many people tell me in interviews, "I quit to focus on a full-time job search." As much as I really want to believe it, this explanation defies human nature. Would *you* give up your paycheck to look for another job, or would you rather keep your job while looking during off hours or after calling in sick to your current job? During the reference check process, I find that the person was either laid off or fired about 80 percent of the time. Even if this person is in the 20 percent of people who really *did* quit their job to focus on searching for a new one, I'm still going to dig into their logic because I'm not sure I like what that says about this person's pragmatism. Knowing when or why someone began a job search is another data point to analyze when you're wondering, "Is this person the right one for this job?"

3. The person quit for some personal reason, or the company went out of business

Sh★t happens, and family tragedies and company implosions are in that category. Be delicate when inquiring about a potential family tragedy, but fire away when it comes to a company implosion. Why did the company fail? What would you have done differently?

There is an additional red flag hiding in all of these questions. Sometimes people extend out their reported dates of employment to cover up gaps so that they can avoid answering these questions. A thorough reference check would catch this misrepresentation. Bonus tip: Be on the lookout for self-employment via "consulting companies" where the job applicant was the CEO and only employee. These are often nonjobs designed to fill employment gaps.

Red Flag 2: No Graduation Date

When candidates fail to provide their graduation date on their resume, I immediately suspect that they are trying to hide their age. Either the candidate is a recent graduate who has a ton of work experience and is afraid to tell people that they're only twenty-two years old, or they're a late-career candidate who's afraid that they'll be seen as too senior for the role. Or, perhaps the person never graduated. If there's no date, I will ask, "In what year did you obtain your degree from XYZ University?"

If their answer indicates that it was awhile ago, I'll follow up by asking about their first job after college and attempt to piece their full work history together. I typically find that candidates who omit graduation dates also omit five to ten years of work experience. If their answer is, "I didn't graduate," and their resume was written to give the appearance that they did, I cut them and move on.

Why do I care about an omitted graduation date? I want to understand why this apparently awesome potential hire feels the need to hide their past. Are they self-conscious about early career choices? Do they think they're overqualified for the job? What are they going to hide from me after I hire them? As an employer, make sure that you obtain and review college transcripts before you make a hiring decision. (We'll talk about other ways to review a candidate's credentials and experience in chapter seven.)

Let me be clear: There is a sharp distinction between uncovering the truth about a candidate's experience and asking them age-related questions. Age discrimination is a shameful and illegal practice, and if you screen based on age, you're going to end up in court on the wrong end of a lawsuit. It also makes you a bad person. Don't do it.

Red Flag 3: Title Creep

When a candidate has clearly embellished the nature and scope of their role to make it sound like they did more than they actually did, that's *title creep*. Long bulleted lists that describe broad responsibilities but omit performance details are a good indication of title creep. For example, a person claiming to be the vice president of product development might say that they managed a team of five designers and led the launch of new products and services. Your resume radar should be sounding alerts at that point, telling you that more details are necessary.

"Describe the team to me. How many of them did you hire personally? Describe the last product launch that you led. What was your specific contribution to that project? What worked well, and what didn't?"

Someone who actually did the job will have a full command of the details.

Red Flag 4: Companies That No Longer Exist

This one is a close relative of Red Flag 1, and occurs whenever you attempt to research a company listed on a candidate's resume and find zero information. If the company listed was Enron or Lehman Brothers, or some such high-profile bankruptcy, fine. But if it's a company that nobody has ever heard of, I want you to start thinking about all of the reasons why no information is available. The most common reason that there are no details about the company is because the company was the candidate's sole proprietorship or small corporation and they dissolved the business. People may be embarrassed to disclose a business failure, but you need to know whether your candidate is comfortable discussing failures. Most entrepreneurs I know wear failures like a badge of honor. Most of them also make terrible employees, which is why they started a company in the first place (it's why I did!).

Red Flag 5: Goofy Resume File Names

This one is my personal favorite. Next time someone sends you an electronic version of their resume, look at the file name. If it's Joe-Smith_Resume.doc, it passes the no goofiness test. If it's titled Joe-Smith_MarketingResume.doc, then you should go into BS detection mode. Why does Joe Smith need to put *marketing resume* in the file name? It's likely that Joe is applying for a bunch of different jobs and is tailoring his resume based on the type of role. I'll bet that Joe also has one called JoeSmith_SalesResume.doc that he uses for sales jobs. This is the one error that most resume cheats don't even realize they're committing. They're just trying to keep all of their resume versions in order using the file name. Keep an eye out for this one—it's subtle but incredibly predictive.

I want to stress that you should presume all candidates are innocent until you have confirmed that they misrepresented themselves on a resume. You will only be able to do that by asking smart, targeted questions asked during the telephone and in-person interview stages. These five red flags can alert you to potential issues and tell you what to focus on. After you've analyzed the first batch of resumes that you've received from your sources, it's time to reach out to those candidates that look qualified for the role.

Making Initial Contact with Job Candidates

The best recruiting processes are scripted events with a defined beginning, middle, and end. Making sure that you know and follow your recruiting script will make the difference between sustained recruiting excellence and haphazard, unpredictable results.

The most effective and efficient way to reach out to job candidates you're interested in is through email.

The layout of this correspondence does three things for you as a hiring manager. First, it lets the candidate know where you found their information. In today's glorious, spam-filled world, people are immediately skeptical of *any* email they get from an unconfirmed or unsolicited source. You need to state right up front the reason for your email. This is also why we put "Your resume/Job opportunity with [Company Name]" as the subject line of the email.

Second, this format provides the candidate with the job title, the timing on the hire, and the location of the position. It then tells them that you're interested in speaking to them because of the information presented in their resume. This approach will prevent candidates who don't meet the timing or location criteria from applying for your job (it saves you time). This approach also gives them some good feelings, which are important in making a positive first impression of you and your company.

Finally, this script asks them to commit to a telephone interview and sets expectations as to its duration. It tells them to set aside a specific block of time and to attach a recent copy of their Word resume. It's also worth noting that email spam filters view attachments as evil, and there is a small chance that certain email hosts could block your emails when you attach a file. If this happens, cut and paste the text of the job description in the body of the email below the signature line, or use a link to the URL where the job description is online. Change the appropriate line to "a link to the job description is included below for your review."

Conducting a Telephone Interview

In seminars and presentations, I like to ask the managers in the audience, "Who at your company personally conducts telephone interviews with their job candidates?"

Typically, about a third of the room raises their hands.

Next I ask, "For those of you who don't conduct telephone screens, what's your reason?"

The overwhelming response? They don't have enough time.

I could tell you that time is money, but as an entrepreneur or business manager, you already know that. If you're like the majority of managers who feel that telephone screens are too time consuming, I'm going to do my best to change your mind. Here are three reasons why the hiring manager—not HR, not anyone else—should personally conduct telephone interviews:

First Contact Email Script

{Subject of email} Your resume / Job opportunity with [Company Name]

Dear [first name],

I recently received your resume from [Indeed/Careerbuilder/Craigslist/your response to our job posting/a recruiter hired by our company] and I'm very interested in speaking with you about your background and experience. As you know, our company is currently looking to hire a [job title] in the [immediate future/next month/next quarter] in [city/location]. Based on the resume I've received, I feel that you may be a good potential fit for this role. A job description is attached for your review.

I'd like to set up a time where we can discuss this role and your experience and career goals in greater detail. I have availability on [Date One] at [Time One] and [Date Two] at [Time Two]. Please let me know which of these times work for you and the best telephone number at which I can reach you. Please set aside about an hour for our conversation.

[Name], I am excited to speak with you and look forward to discussing this opportunity with you in greater detail. Please attach the most-recent Word copy of your resume with your reply.

Best regards,
[You]

1. You have accountability for the entire process

If you push telephone interviews off on someone else in your business, you give away control of the crucial first interview in the hiring process to someone who doesn't have anywhere near the vested interest that you do in hiring the right person for the job. It's your hire, it's your new employee, and it's your rear end that's on the line to produce results. You need to be the one selecting spot-on employees for your team. The manager with the open position should be the one who conducts the telephone screen. *Period.* It's the only way to ensure that the process is truly owned. As an added bonus, when it's your company's midlevel managers hiring for their open roles, you can teach them how to evaluate and choose talent—an important skill for all leaders.

The only time that you should let someone else conduct a phone interview is when you have a verifiably awesome talent acquisition professional on your payroll, someone whose entire existence depends on creating a predictable pipeline of quality candidates. If you have such a person on your team, and they've earned your trust with their ability to assess talent, get your quality prospects excited about your opportunity, and set your managers up for recruiting success, then by all means—delegate.

2. You promote and reinforce a culture of excellence

Companies should start their telephone interviews with the following script:

Hello, Jane? This is Adam Robinson calling from ABC Incorporated. Thanks for setting some time aside to talk with me about our open position. Before we begin, I'd like to take a few minutes to walk you through our selection process because it's probably a lot more in-depth than you're accustomed to.

Our company takes performance management very seriously, and we're committed to hiring the absolute best people out there to join our team. The first step in the process is this one—the telephone interview. Our goal for the next [15/30/60] minutes is to learn about you and talk about your career experience at a high level. I also want to give you an opportunity to learn more about our open position. At the end of this call, we should both know whether or not this opportunity is a good mutual fit. If it is, we'll invite you in to meet with me and other members of my team. We'll follow that up with a second in-person interview. If at that point we're still all in agreement that this is a great mutual fit, we'll ask you to set up reference calls for each of your direct supervisors from the past ten years. All told, the process should take about [one/two/three weeks] from start to finish.

That might sound like a really involved process—it is. The upside to our employees is that we surround ourselves with great people who are as committed to high performance as we are. We want to be a hundred percent sure that we hire people who are a great fit both culturally and professionally. Does that approach sound okay to you? Great, well then let's start by discussing your high-level career goals . . .

This script takes about a minute to say, but it has far-reaching benefits that will help you build a world-class team. The first thing this script does is to set a professional tone. The tone signals that you, as a hiring manager, have your proverbial stuff together. Second, the script telegraphs your hiring process. The candidate is now fully aware that he or she will be going through a multistep process and knows that you'll be checking references. Less than ideal candidates will often back out of the process right here on the spot, knowing that their chances of getting hired are slim. Finally, this script communicates to the candidate that your company has a culture of

performance. Great people want to work with other ¡
The best candidates will be totally fired up to be speaₙᵢₙg
company who understands what it means to promote excellence.
Remember—star performers *always* have their choice of job opportunities. You need to make your firm stand out from all of the others.
Offering them an opportunity to work for a company governed as a
meritocracy is a great way to do it.

3. You save yourself a ton of time over the long run

If you skip the telephone interview and go straight to the in-person
interview, you're going to end up spending a lot of time talking to
people who will demonstrate in the first few minutes that they are not
the right fit. You can end a telephone call in ten minutes and not look
like a total jerk, but cutting off a personal interview in ten minutes
is downright rude. Ever spend thirty minutes talking to a candidate
who might as well have walked in randomly off the street? How many
times did you look at your watch while you imagined your inbox
filling up with unread email, hoping that someone would come along
and put you out of your misery?

When conducted properly, a telephone screen will weed out 75
percent of your original candidate pool. Your goal is to take the top 25
percent into the first round of personal interviews. The phone interview creates internal accountability, promotes a culture of excellence,
and saves you hours of wasted interviews.

If I have convinced you to start screening your candidates, it's time
to talk about the techniques you can use to make the phone interview
a successful experience.

The Six Elements of a Telephone Interview

Consistency is key when conducting telephone interviews. You want to make sure that you follow the same script for every candidate so that you eliminate variables from your interview process. Follow this comprehensive outline when conducting a telephone interview:

1. Start with an Introduction

A proper introduction is important in any interview situation, and telephone-based interviews are no different. You'll start by introducing yourself (genius, I know) and thanking the candidate for setting time aside to speak with you. Then, you'll take a minute to walk the candidate through your company's interview process. Finally, you'll say a few words about the importance of performance management to your organization and confirm the candidate's acceptance of the overall approach.

2. Discuss the Candidate's Career Plan

You'll begin the interview portion of the conversation by discussing the candidate's career plan. Asking a candidate to talk about their career goals is a nonthreatening way to break the ice and put your interviewee at ease. If you dive right into their resume (as approximately 99 percent of other interviewers do) you'll get programmed answers that tell you what they think you want to hear. We're looking for authenticity. Ask them their twenty-year, five-year, and one-year professional goals. You'll get a good overview of your candidate and a good sense of their vision for themselves.

3. Discover What They're Best At and Don't Like

This is my favorite part of the telephone interview. After discussing the candidate's career plan, you're going to ask them two questions.

First, ask them what they think they're best at, professionally speaking, and what type of work they enjoy doing. This begins a career audit trail that shows you the type of work this person excels at. Then, you'll ask the candidate what type of work they *don't* like doing. These answers tend to be things that the candidate will be less good at, but we'll verify that down the road in the personal interview (should the candidate make it to that point). My experience has taught me that people enjoy work that they're good at and tend to dislike things that they're not as good at.

The moral of the story is that if the person tells you that they're great at performing the type of work that you'll need them to perform in your open role, they're in good shape—so far. If you're looking to hire for an administrative position and the candidate tells you that they "hate doing paperwork," you're probably wise to cut them at the telephone interview. This approach is a good spot-check to make sure all parties are on the same page.

4. Explore the Candidate's Job History

Notice that we don't start talking about the candidate's job experience until the midpoint of the interview. Why? If their career plan and what they are best at and don't like aren't a good fit for the role that you're trying to fill, does job history matter? This part of the interview isn't the typical, "Tell me about your role at *XYZ* company" approach that you're probably used to; save those questions for the in-person interview. Instead, ask a few simple questions about each experience listed on their resume, in reverse chronological order:

- Why did you decide to join *XYZ* Company?

- What are/were you accountable for in this role, in specific and measurable terms?

- How will they rate your performance when we talk with them, and why?

We ask in reverse chronological order because candidates are a lot more comfortable talking about their job ten years ago than they are talking about their current boss. So by the time you work your way up to their current or latest role, they've already given up the goods on every previous job. They will likely answer your questions about their current job because it would seem odd not to divulge this information after how frank they have been with their other positions.

5. Discuss the Open Position

You should talk about the open position by reading a summary of the role from the job profile that you created, and then ask the candidate whether or not they feel that they're a good fit. Ask them if anything they've learned about the job or the company thus far gives them cause for concern. Thankfully, weaker candidates, having been called to task on previous employers and job experience, will many times take this opportunity to tell you that they're not a good fit.

6. Wrap Up the Interview and Outline the Next Steps

Cap off the interview with four questions. You'll know by their answers whether or not your candidate is truly interested and available for employment with your company:

- What's your timeline for making a decision on a new job?
- Do you have any offers pending that will make it hard for you to complete our hiring process?
- As you evaluate your next move, what things are most important to you?

- Is there anything that you feel is relevant to our conversation that we haven't yet discussed?

All told, this interview can last fifteen minutes to an hour, depending on how many follow-up questions you have for the candidate's responses. With this approach, you get much more than the typical exercise of reading through a resume together. You begin to get inside the candidate's head and start to learn what makes them tick. These are the data points you need to make a truly informed decision.

Making a Go/No-Go Call after a Telephone Interview

The telephone interview has a singular goal: to determine whether or not the candidate should be granted a personal interview. The phone screening approach that I teach is designed to elicit the information that you need to make this decision. Let's take a closer look at the must-get information from such a call and analyze how you decide whether or not someone should move to the next stage:

Analyzing the Introduction for Behavioral Clues

This is one of two points in the conversation at which you should be talking more than 10 percent of the time; the other is when you are reading the job profile. Unless your candidate commits an egregious affront to common decency such as chronic interruptions or overt disinterest in what you're saying, then you probably won't give too much thought to this part of the interview.

Evaluating the Candidate's Career Plan

In this section, the candidate will give you the road map that they've created for themselves. This road map may be incredibly detailed, with clear milestones and objectives, and an impressive level of specificity. If this is the case, it's time to think about what they've told you. Does the opportunity that you're presenting line up with their one-year and five-year career plan? Do you see a major divergence between the career path you're offering and the career plan that they've discussed with you?

The most common red flag at this stage can be if the hiring manager realizes that their company can't deliver the career path that the candidate desires. Most managers pay lip service to the candidate's five-year plan and then promptly forget what's been told to them. Instead, ask yourself, "Can my company help this candidate grow, given what I've just learned about their career plan?"

Many factors can explain why the average tenure of a degreed professional in the United States is less than three years, and a company failing to understand an employee's career needs is at the top of that list. Although talking about your candidate's career plan helps point out obvious disconnects between your open position and the candidate's plan, don't pass up this opportunity to understand your candidate. You'll be a more effective manager if you have this information up front.

Considering What the Candidate Is Best At or Doesn't Like

The answers to these questions are of paramount concern. The more of these telephone interviews that you conduct, the more you'll begin to recognize patterns of behavior across the career histories of your candidates. The ability to uncover what your candidate is best at or doesn't like is *the most important skill* you need to develop. Without this skill, the rest of the process is suspect. Nothing else matters if you're offering a job that the candidate either doesn't want to do or isn't very good at doing. This is where they'll tell you whether or not that's the case.

In many respects, people are pretty easy to read. We have preferences about the type of work that we like to do, and most of us do better work when we enjoy the work we're doing. What's also generally true is that we are better at some things than others, and there are certain types of work that we really dislike. People tend to not enjoy doing work that they're not good at. If someone tells you that they're terrified of making cold calls, then don't hire them as a salesperson where 90 percent of their leads will be coming from their own outbound cold-calling efforts. Yet, these misfit hires happen all the time.

If what a candidate's best at matches a core competency of your open position, proceed. Conversely, if they don't like a core element of your open position—Houston, we have a problem.

Reading the Candidate's Job History

The Hireology approach to discussing job history is different from the conventional approach that most entrepreneurs and business managers are accustomed to using. We don't spend time asking candidates about what they did at ACME Incorporated; instead we immediately ask them *why* they decided to work for ACME Incorporated. What we're looking for is something we call an *interview tell*. Most of us are familiar with reading someone when playing a game like poker. In poker speak, a *tell* is a way of acting or speaking that gives away a person's true motive or disposition. In hiring speak, an interview tell is a way of acting or speaking that tells a hiring manager that the candidate's answer was less accurate or truthful than they would have us believe.

You can observe a number of common interview tells when you ask in the interview, "What were you accountable for doing on a day-to-day basis, and what were your major accomplishments during your time there?" If the candidate was a top performer and knows it, then the candidate's answer will be immediate and full of details. If the candidate says something like, "I can't recall the details, exactly, it was a long time ago," it's a huge red flag.

Another common interview tell comes when you ask your candidate why they made the decision to leave an employer listed on their resume (or their current one). A lack of specificity, often in the form of an answer like, "It was time for me to move on, I learned all that I could" or "I needed a new challenge" can sometimes mean "I didn't get along with my boss and got pushed out" or "I quit before they could fire me."

This isn't a polygraph exam, folks. They're just data points, albeit important ones. And at Hireology we're collecting as many of them as we can. Great employees have a command of the details of their former jobs. Mediocre employees typically don't. The telephone interview will likely tell you which type of potential employee you're dealing with.

Reviewing the Candidate's Reading of Your Open Position

Just as you analyzed the behavior of the candidate during your introduction, watch them for social miscues like interruptions when you discuss the basics of the open position.

Wrapping Up the Interview and the Candidate's Next Steps

The answers to these questions are relevant only if you've decided to move forward with the candidate. If they're a go, then these questions are crucial to your understanding of what will drive their decision to choose an employer. If they're a no-go, these questions are compulsory but not material. Cut your losses.

- "What's your timeline for making a decision on a new job?"

  If you get a firm answer: good. Wishy-washy answer: less good.

- "Do you have any offers pending that will make it hard for you to complete our four-week interview process?"

  Firm answer with detail and specificity: good. Wishy-washy answer: less good.

- "As you evaluate your next move, what things are most important to you?"

  Firm, reasonable answer: good. Uncertainty or unreasonable answer: less good.

- "Is there anything that you feel is relevant to our conversation that we haven't yet discussed?"

  Pointed questions about your company that demonstrate this person's interest and preparedness: good. Anything else: depends.

  You're not going to figure out everything there is to know about a candidate with a one-hour telephone interview. You can, however, learn enough to make a go or no-go decision and save yourself a ton of time.

  Once you have used this screening process to identify promising candidates, it's time to schedule in-person interviews.

Case Study: Hiring with Patience

As the founder of a fast-growing business, hiring is always a challenge. Just ask Tim Heitmann, who started Popcorn Palace, a business that provides some twenty flavors of gourmet popcorn but with a twist. Rather than sell through retail channels, Popcorn Palace provides its product to organizations that then use the popcorn to raise money for various causes. Heitmann's company, which is based in Burr Ridge, IL, has since made the prestigious Inc. 5000 list, which recognizes the fastest-growing private companies in the US, an impressive *ten times* in a row.

Today, Heitmann says his organization has fifty full-time employees, with another twenty or so who join on to help handle the holiday rush. When he first got started, Heitmann admits that his interview process for new hires lasted all of ten minutes.

"We were always in a rush to fill that open seat," says Heitmann.

Making fast decisions might have helped him fill open positions in the short term, but Heitmann now realizes he likely put his company at risk by potentially making bad hires. Heitmann remembers one senior-level hire he made when, almost immediately after he made the hire, he realized it was a mistake.

"He wasn't a toxic employee, but he clearly wasn't a good cultural fit," Heitmann says.

Heitmann admits to keeping the person on the payroll for two years because he thought it would be a greater hassle to try and replace him than to have him continue to work. Today, Heitmann wonders what opportunities his company might have been able to pursue if he had the right person on board all along.

"The ripple effect of making a bad hiring decision could be disastrous for some companies," Heitmann says.

He has since learned to be patient when it comes to filling his open positions to help ensure that whoever comes on board is a great cultural fit.

One way that Heitmann has improved his hiring process while slowing it down is by engaging multiple people from his business in the hiring process to help ensure hard-to-quantify elements like cultural fit.

Case in point: When he wanted to hire a new chief marketing officer (CMO), Heitmann brought in a high-profile candidate who had a rockstar resume and experience working with big corporations. Heitmann enlisted two managers who would be reporting to the new CMO as part of the interview process. When Heitmann asked them for their input after the interviews—he was sold on hiring the candidate—his managers told him they didn't like her.

"They told me that they had some very serious concerns about what it would be like to work for her," says Heitmann. "They thought she was arrogant and not humble enough."

Heitmann knew this person was an A-caliber player, a star performer who was capable of transforming his organization. He was torn: He thought he should hire the candidate, but he was unsure.

As it happened, Heitmann was headed on a trip to India and he told the candidate he would likely make her an offer when he got back. As he traveled, he couldn't shake what he'd heard from his managers—the people who would be working with the new CMO on a daily basis. When he returned, he made the decision to not hire the superstar. The risk that she could rip the organization's culture apart was too big.

"I called her up and told her it just wasn't the right fit," Heitmann says.

In a case of serendipity, another candidate came to Heitmann's attention a couple weeks later—someone who turned out to be an amazing fit for the organization.

"If I had hired the other person, I don't believe we could have accomplished everything that we have been able to do with the second candidate," says Heitmann.

This experience, he says, proves the value of involving multiple people in the hiring process and taking your time to make the best possible choice.

"Fighting the rush to hire someone probably takes the most discipline when it comes to hiring—especially in fast-growing companies," says Heitmann.

· · ·

CHAPTER SUMMARY

People often inflate or misrepresent work experience on their resumes. You need to develop a process to identify red flags and inconsistencies as you begin to whittle down your pool of candidates to those you want to interview.

You should personally reach out to the candidates you are interested in with an initial telephone screening. This isn't a job to delegate. If you make the time now and follow a script, you'll be speaking with more qualified and motivated candidates during your next round of in-person interviews.

SELF-ANALYSIS

Ask yourself the following questions:

- What is your process for screening resumes?

- As a leader, do you take part in the initial candidate screening process? Why or why not?

- Do you have a script to follow to ensure that you are screening every candidate in the same way? Are you putting yourself at risk for wasted time if you don't?

KEY TAKEAWAYS

1 Develop a rock-solid screening process to identify candidate red flags as early as possible.

2 Make an initial phone screen, using a script, the first step in your hiring process. You'll save yourself wasted time in the long run.

3 Identify the key elements that will establish whether a candidate is a go or a no-go after that initial screening call.

Chapter Six

DIG DEEPER

Most entreprencurs and business managers don't conduct interviews. Instead, they have conversations. When a job candidate comes for an in-person interview, managers and entrepreneurs talk about how great their business and their employees are. They talk about the growth prospects, their client list, and how they made the Inc. 500 list last year. The manager tells the candidate how much they would love working there. Meanwhile the candidate sits, smiling and nodding, listening to the hiring manager gush. Inevitably, the manager will stop, look at the candidate, and say, "So, enough about us. Why do you want to work here?"

The candidate then repeats back everything the manager just said, parroting the hiring manager's reasons for wanting the position. The manager and the candidate banter back and forth until time runs out. The candidate leaves, excited about the company, but not exactly sure what the job entails. The manager leaves, excited about the candidate, but without a clue about how the person would perform.

Later, the manager extends an offer, the candidate accepts it, and six months afterward the manager and the candidate are both frustrated because neither one understood or managed their expectations. Does this scenario sound familiar?

Most people are nice, and people want to connect with others. Entrepreneurs are accustomed to informality, and that casualness translates into their interview style. The result is an interview approach that goes a long way toward building rapport but falls short of eliciting information that predicts the candidate's success.

To correct this problem, enter what I call the *talent mindset*. The talent mindset is the hiring manager's version of being in the zone. It's a mental preparation that readies you, the hiring manager, for having an engaging and productive interview with your candidate. How do you know you're in the talent mindset?

1. You're prepared

The first step in creating a talent mindset is *preparation*. If you have to fumble around for the right questions to ask, you're not going to have a good interview. By contrast, if you only have to ask questions and listen, you've set up an ideal situation.

2. You're comfortable

Most of us don't like judging others. Fight the urge to be everyone's friend; it will destroy your ability to conduct a solid interview. It's hard for many of us to objectively find fault in others, especially if they're likeable. Get into the talent mindset so you are ready to judge the abilities and accomplishments of another person. Understand that your mission is to determine whether or not this person will succeed in your open role. We're not choosing friends. Hiring mistakes cost a lot of money.

3. You're protective

A company culture takes years to create, but one bad hire can throw it into total meltdown. Many of us have had the experience of knowing on a new employee's first day that we've made a hiring mistake, because two or three of our employees are visibly disturbed when speaking to them (and perhaps have even told us so). Being in the talent mindset means *guarding* your company's culture like the irreplaceable asset that it is. If you're going to create a company full of superstars, you can't let a single bad apple into the barrel. Protect your company's culture as if it were the most important part of your job, because it is.

Before you conduct your next in-person interview, walk through the following questions to determine if you're in the talent mindset: Am I prepared for this interview? Am I ready to judge another person? Am I approaching this interview as a guardian of my company's culture?

If the answers are yes, you've set yourself up for interviewing and hiring success.

The In-Depth Interview

After you've interviewed enough applicants through your telephone interviews to yield three to five viable candidates, you've completed the first round of your hiring process. Now, you carry forward the best candidates for the second round. At this point, you should be reasonably certain that these candidates would likely perform well in the open role. The goal of the second interview is to find out which of your candidates will have the highest likelihood of success. This stage is where we attempt to poke around inside the candidate's head and find out what makes them tick. This is how you'll identify the candidate to take forward to the next step.

I recommend scheduling one in-person interview per day on consecutive days. This schedule keeps you in the talent mindset and makes it easier for you to compare and contrast results. You should budget approximately two hours for each interview to give your team and the candidate ample time. Once the interview begins, set the stage, get the candidate a beverage of their choice, and create a positive, relaxed tone. By this stage of the interview process, you will have talked with your candidate in some detail during the phone screen, so it should be easy to establish rapport. If you are struggling to connect with your candidate during the second interview, I'd have some serious concerns about cultural fit.

Unlike the telephone screen, the second round should be conducted with an interview buddy. You, as the hiring manager, should ask the questions, while your interview buddy listens intently and takes notes. As you'll soon discover, the interview questions employed in the second round are much deeper and thought provoking than simple job-related inquiries. I mention this point because in the in-person interview, your interview buddy will have a lot of content to absorb and they'll need to prepare accordingly.

The questions that you'll ask in this interview will all be pre-scripted. Everything you're going to ask will be determined ahead of time. You'll ask the same questions, in the same order, with each and every candidate. Most hiring managers have difficulty with interviews because they're unsure of what to ask. As a result, each interview is different and produces no baseline for comparison. The hiring manager is then left to select the best candidates with guess-work and gut feelings.

To prevent this situation from happening, ask the same questions of each candidate, *regardless of the role and regardless of their level of experience.* The context of the role (entry level versus senior level) will not necessitate a change in the question format, but the answers from candidates *will* be commensurate with the context of the role. No need to change the script for each and every position—a real time-saver and one less thing for you to worry about! Plus, when you're not fumbling around for the next question to ask, you can focus on listening to your candidate. It's amazing what you'll learn!

The second-round interview script presented here is based on the core competencies that form the basis of the Hireology Intelligent Hiring Platform. The script has multiple questions for each competency and elicits information from the candidate so that you, the hiring manager, can determine the candidate's level of competency. Will they or won't they be a good fit for your role? This interview will tell you everything you need to know.

Accept no candidate response at face value. It's not a candidate's initial answer to your question that matters most. It's the answers to your follow-up questions that yield the real substance in this interview. To dig more deeply in this way, simply say, "Tell me a bit more about that" after the candidate's initial response. Then watch what happens. Then ask it again. And then again. Ask it three times, every time. Here's what a typical exchange might look like:

You: What's the greatest asset that you'll bring to our company?

Candidate: My biggest asset is my ability to build new relationships with prospects. I will be able to break new accounts for you and bring in a ton of new revenue.

You: Tell me more about that.

Candidate: Well, I'm really good at making cold calls. In my last company, I didn't have any lead generation support and had to rely on myself to make things happen.

You: That's great. Tell me more about that.

Candidate: Well, the company didn't really have a marketing department, and the president of the company told me to do whatever I needed to do to generate sales. I relied on an approach that worked really well for me in the past—cold calling. I made around a hundred cold calls each and every day.

You: Tell me more about that. Was this approach successful?

Candidate: It was incredibly successful. As you can see from my resume, I was able to meet quota every quarter for nine consecutive quarters using nothing but cold calling. Now, it's not my favorite approach to sales, but if it's what's necessary, I'm willing to do it to be successful.

What a difference it makes asking candidates to tell you more, right? Instead of moving on to the next question after learning nothing substantive about your candidate, you now know that this person can likely crank out cold calls in an environment without any marketing support. What if you found out that this candidate was previously successful because they had a ton of lead generation support but your position would require a hundred cold calls a day with zero marketing support? Would that person be successful in your role? Maybe, maybe not. We now know the likelihood of "maybe not" has increased substantially.

The goal of the second round of interviews is to determine the *one* candidate who is most likely to succeed in your open position. You should enter this stage of the interview process with this result in mind.

How to Conduct an In-Person Candidate Interview

Now that we've talked about preparing for the second, in-person round of candidate interviews, let's take a look at the scripted part of this interview and the high-level topical questions that you'll want to ask a candidate. These questions should be asked in order, without any skipping around. Remember—consistency is key when you're setting a baseline for candidate assessment.

After everyone has been seated, you should open the interview with the following scripted intro:

Thanks for setting aside this time to come in and visit with us about our open role. We've been impressed with what we've learned about you thus far, and I want you to know that you're now a finalist for the [open position title] role here at [company name]. When we first met on the phone, I explained to you that we have a thorough interview process, and I want to again thank you for understanding how important choosing the right person for this job is to our company and its culture.

In this interview, we're going to talk about more high-level topics, as opposed to the last interview where we primarily focused on specific job experience. I'd like for you to relax and prepare to think big picture. Our goal here is to get a good sense of who you are, what motivates you, and how we can best help you to achieve your career goals, should you join our firm. But before we begin, are there any questions that you have about this process thus far?

Then, we can begin by diving right into the first questions.

Questions to Check the Performance Results Competencies

Ask the following questions to check the two Performance Results competencies.

Quality of Work

1 "Over the course of your career, what role has quality played in your overall performance?"

This is a wide-open question designed to tell you whether or not this candidate understands the influence of quality on job performance. Can they explain how quality—of product delivery, service delivery, or some other output—translates to their individual accomplishments?

2 "What standards and procedures for delivering work are/were in place in your current/most recent position?"

The answer to this question will tell you whether or not this candidate's accomplishments were the result of following a process or winging it. There is *no wrong answer* here. The answer must be evaluated in terms of *your* company's internal workings. If you are extremely process oriented, and this candidate demonstrates that they have been previously successful because of their ability to improvise, you may have a bad fit. If, on the other hand, your company has no documented processes, then someone who can succeed in a "just wing it!" environment may be the perfect fit.

Quantity of Work

1 "What have you done on your last/present position to increase your organization's top-line revenues?"

Let's find out if this candidate understands how their performance ties to revenue. It's possible for every position in every company. Again, no wrong answers here. If your role requires someone who sees the big picture, then a detailed answer to this question is probably a must-have. On the other hand, if you've determined that you need a heads-down administrative resource, and the candidate tells you that they're not sure how they tied into revenue generation, then it was probably a miss to begin with.

2 "How many hours a week do you find it necessary to work to get your job done?"

This question will provide all sorts of opportunity for follow-ups. If the answer is forty hours, what did they do that made them able to leave at five p.m. every day? Did they not have enough to do, or was it just that they were organized? If they answer something like eighty hours, does this person have an organization or prioritization problem? Are they a workaholic? Do they take on too much work?

3 "What kinds of deadlines did/do you deal with in your last/present job?"

We want to get a sense of the time-driven pressure that this person has faced. Were they reasonable deadlines? What was the workload?

4 "Have you ever been asked to accept additional responsibilities or work at a time when you were already maxed out?"

There's a lot of food for thought in the responses to this one. Is this the type of person who's inclined to assist the team when asked, no matter their workload? Or is this person hesitant to jump in when their plate is already full?

Questions to Check Performance Factor Competencies

The interview now moves to the Performance Factors competencies.

Job Knowledge and Technical Application

1 "Describe to me the specific things you know and have experience with that enable you to succeed in your job."

Does this candidate truly understand what makes them successful in their role? Can they articulate it well?

2 "Tell me about the last professional training or education that you received."

Top professionals are motivated to learn. Find out how often the candidate took advantage of learning opportunities. If they didn't have a chance to receive professional training, either through their employer or on their own . . . why?

3 "Give me an example of how you use current information about the industry to increase performance in your role."

Are they someone who takes new information and employs it to their advantage?

Organization and Planning

1 "How organized are you?"

Another question with no right answer, just something that you want to know to assess job and cultural fit.

2 "I'd like for you to think about the last project or assignment that you worked on where you had tight deadlines and multiple milestones. Describe it to me."

Rarely will people come out and tell you that they're unorganized, but resources who pride themselves on their organization will go out of their way to describe their system to you. That's what you're listening for.

Analytics and Problem Solving

1 "Describe your process for analyzing a problem that needs to be solved."

Does this person approach a problem systematically, or do they just start hammering away at it? Neither one is bad, but you certainly want to know which approach they use!

2 "What was the last problem that you had to solve on the job?"

Sure, they can talk about problem solving, but can they tell you about a specific problem they solved?

3 "Tell me about a time when you anticipated a problem and prevented it from becoming a problem by taking preemptive action."

Another question that asks them to demonstrate their qualifications. Find out if they can walk the walk. The best answers here demonstrate an understanding of the bigger picture, requiring them to step in before a situation got ugly.

Judgment and Decision Making

1 "Describe the last time you had to make a decision between two courses of action and dealt with significant consequences?"

You may get a personal response to this one (it happens about one in three times I ask it). These answers can get pretty deep. Be prepared to listen actively.

2 "Have you ever made a decision at work that turned out to be the wrong one?"

We all make decisions that turned out to be the wrong one. Yes, even you. What did they learn from this mistake? What would they do differently the next time?

3 "Describe your decision-making process."

Are they more from the gut, or do they tend to gather information and analyze it first? To what degree do they involve additional team members, or managers, in their decision?

4 "What was the last mistake that you made?"

This is another question that may elicit a personal answer. In one very memorable interview I had a candidate tell me that getting married again was the last mistake they made.

"When did you get married again?" I asked.
"Last week."
Ouch. (Be careful with marriage–related questions in the interview!)

Self-Improvement and Initiative

I "What professional organizations are you involved with?"

Do they participate in relevant professional organizations or societies? People who participate in extracurricular groups or activities tend to be better networked, which has all sorts of positive benefits for them and for their employer.

2 "How do you stay current with knowledge?"

Is this someone who invests in keeping skills and knowledge sharp? Are they a self-described lifelong learner? Do they believe in the concept of continuous learning, and back it up with actions?

3 "Describe the last constructive feedback that you received from your manager."

We're trying to get a preview of what we'll find in the reference check. The answer to this question will likely line up with the candidate's pattern of behavior that you have observed over the last two interviews, and, not coincidentally, with the things that they've told us they don't enjoy doing.

Innovation and Creativity

I "Do you consider yourself a creative person?"

You'll be surprised how many people tell you, "Not really." It's not a bad answer, unless you're hiring for a design role. In that case, this question may be a bit goofy to ask. Ask it anyway.

2 "Describe a time when you created a new way of doing things at work."

Is this person someone who's comfortable challenging the status quo? Do they think creatively about new approaches to issues or problems?

3   "Have you ever spoken up about something you knew wasn't working as well as it could?"

This question will give you a clue as to whether or not they actually tell people about their ideas when they have them. It's also an indication of assertiveness.

4   "Are you more of a detail-oriented person or a big-picture person?"

No wrong answers; only bad job fits. Don't put a blue-sky thinker in a role where they are poring through data ten hours a day, or making one hundred sales calls.

Questions to Check the Candidate's Interpersonal Skill Competencies

The Interpersonal Skill competencies have several subcategories: communication, teamwork, and supervision.

Communication

1   "Describe your communication style."

Are they more authoritarian or collaborative in approach? Does this person understand their communication style well enough to explain it to you?

2   "What kind of written documentation do you regularly produce for your last/present role?"

I will say it again—don't put someone who has never written detailed and frequent reports in a role that requires detailed and written report writing as a crucial component of success.

3 "On a scale of one to ten, with ten being highest, how would you describe your ability to write articulately in English?"

Are they a good speller? Do they like to write? Ever read an email that one of your employees has written to a customer and then winced because of the horrendous grammar? Better to find out now.

4 "Describe your approach to dealing with internal and external clients."

Is it effective? Does their approach mirror the one your company takes? Can you find any bad habits that you'll need to break?

5 "Describe a time when you've had to modify your communication style to get through to someone, either at work or with a customer."

This is one of those questions that yield answers all over the map. The conflicts discussed will range from benign to full-blown mayhem. With this question, it's important to dig for details. What was the conflict or situation that created the need for creative communication? What specific approach did they take, and how did it impact the result?

6 "If we asked you to stand up and give an extemporaneous speech in front of hundreds of people, how comfortable would you be?"

Here we're trying to determine their self-rated level of comfort with public speaking. Most people are terrified of public speaking. If the role requires speaking in front of large groups of people, then the answer to this question is important. Otherwise, this answer may not be relevant.

Teamwork

1 "Describe your current team."

You might even ask them to draw you an organizational chart. Great follow-up questions include, "Which of these team members were there when you started?" and "Which of these team members are top performers, in your opinion? Why/why not?"

2 "Have you ever been on a team where there is open conflict?"

If yes, make sure it wasn't your candidate who was the source of it. Dig into the details by probing with consecutive "tell me more about that" statements. Think about the team that they'll be joining at your firm, and decide what kind of person will likely succeed.

3 "Are you a 'people person'?"

Nearly everyone will say yes. Then ask, "Given your choice, would you prefer to work with others or work solo?"

There's your real answer.

4 "Do you consider yourself to be a natural leader of people?"

One needs not be extroverted to consider themselves a leader of people. I've found that introverts will describe themselves as natural leaders when it comes to leading by example. Engineers can lead with code quality, accountants with attention to detail, etc.

5 "When was the last time that someone at work asked you for help?"

Do coworkers see this candidate as a resource? Was this a major help request, indicating a high level of trust, or a minor request, positive but less impactful?

6 "When was the last time you asked for help at work?"

Does this person ask for help when they need it? Did they need a major bailout? If so, can they describe how they ended up in that situation?

Supervision

1 "Describe your previous/current manager."

Do they describe him/her in a positive light or a negative one?

2 "How does your manager stay up-to-date on what you're doing?"

Is this person micromanaged or allowed to roam free? How does that compare to your style?

3 "What's your definition of micromanagement?"

Is it a reasonable definition? Some workers believe that any level of metrics-driven supervision qualifies as micromanagement.

4 "Who's the best boss you've ever had?"

Great question. Find out which management style works best for them.

5 "Who's the worst boss you've ever had?"

Another great question! Find out what management style doesn't work with this candidate. Hopefully, it's not your style, too.

Determine the Candidate's X-Factor with Your Final Questions

The last questions deal with what I call the *X-Factor.* In hiring, the X-factor refers to the intangibles that contribute to a candidate's likelihood of success but don't fit neatly into any of the competencies described previously. Things you need to know:

1 "Tell me about your greatest strength and why it will benefit our company."

Similar to the answer to the "best at/don't like" questions on the telephone interview, the answer to this question will help you better understand what this person enjoys doing and believes they're good at. I recommend adding a "why it will benefit our company" modifier to demonstrate the degree the candidate is connecting their abilities with the needs of your company and the specific job they're interviewing for.

2 "What one area do you really need to work on in your career to become more effective on a day-to-day basis?"

Again, we're triangulating with another version of "best at/don't like" to connect the dots. The answer to this question will yield valuable insights and provide you with another approach vector to determine where the candidate sees themselves as potentially deficient.

3 "What was the best job you ever had?"

The actual job itself is not what's important. You are going to probe the answer with smart follow-ups and dig into *why* this job was their choice. Was it the manager? The team? The culture of the company? Fast growth? Financial rewards? What you'll learn translates into the professional values system of your potential hire. Do they line up with yours and that of your organization?

4 "What's the worst job you've ever had?"

You're asking this question for all of the same reasons outlined above, and you're digging for the same information to understand root causes behind their choice. Pay close attention to the events and circumstances that led to this "worst job ever" classification.

Wow, this is a lot of stuff to ask, right? I've made this list so that you can break the interview into hour chunks and let multiple interview teams handle these different sessions separately. Multiple teams and sessions are a great way for you to include other team members in the process (teach great interviewing skills to your future leaders!). Or, you plow through the whole thing in one sitting with a single, diverse team. It's your choice.

Skills and Personality Testing

As we've discussed throughout this book, a great hiring process is all about managing risk. No matter how extensively you interview a candidate, it's still possible that you might have missed something that could lead you to make a poor hiring decision. It's worth adding another line of defense: skills and personality testing.

Testing Is Not a Silver Bullet

Hiring managers try to use personality profiling and job fit assessments as the ultimate source of truth. Their approach goes something like, "I'll just give everyone this assessment, and candidates who score a certain profile type will be hired. Everyone who doesn't score this profile type will be out of luck."

There are no shortcuts when it comes to creating a predictive hiring process. No single test or assessment exists that, when used as the sole basis of evaluation, can consistently and accurately produce the right answer on a hiring decision. It might surprise you to hear someone in my field of work say this, but in my experience the over-reliance on testing as a hiring tool has caused subpar results for the organizations that use it.

The research on this topic illuminates the challenges facing managers when they rely on personality assessments as the sole basis for their hiring decisions. The authors of an article in *Human Resources Management*[13] surveyed a thousand members of the Society for Human Resource Management (SHRM). The people surveyed were human resource managers, directors, and vice presidents that had an average of fourteen years' experience.

The researchers found that even highly experienced HR professionals struggle to understand how to effectively measure job fit using testing and assessments. The following chart is a list of *untrue* statements, along with the corresponding percentage of HR professionals who believe—incorrectly—that the statement is true.

13   Sara L. Rynes, Amy E. Colbert, Kenneth G. Brown, "HR Professionals' Beliefs About Effective Human Resource Practices: Correspondence Between Research And Practice," *Human Resource Management* 41, no. 2 (Summer 2002): 149–174.

FIG 6.1—WHAT HR MANAGERS GET WRONG ABOUT HIRING RESEARCH

% Answering Incorrectly	Belief Statement
84%	Companies that screen for values have better performance than those that screen for intelligence
82%	Conscientiousness is a better predictor of job performance than intelligence
69%	Integrity tests have high degrees of adverse impact
68%	Integrity tests are not very effective in practice because so many people lie on them
58%	Being very intelligent is actually a disadvantage for performing well on a low-skilled job
58%	Being intelligent is a disadvantage in low-skilled jobs
51%	There are four basic personality dimesions, like in MBTI

If even seasoned HR professionals can be wrong, what's a business manager to do? The key is to focus on measuring the right things.

What Are the Most Effective Screening Approaches?

Extensive research has been performed on whether hiring tools can accurately predict job performance. In 2013, researcher Frank Schmidt updated his 1998 analysis of over a hundred years of workplace productivity data to determine the validity of many commonly used assessment practices. What he found is outlined in the following chart:

FIG 6.2–THE MOST EFFECTIVE HIRING SELECTION METHODS

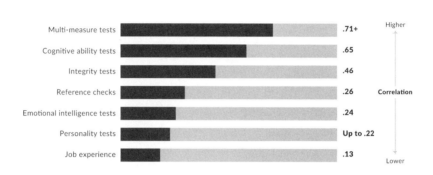

These results produce the following insight: If you are using just one type of assessment like a personality profile, you are choosing to use a process that is *significantly less effective* than if multiple effective measures were incorporated. Managers who want to employ testing to improve their ability to hire should employ a multimeasure approach that tests multiple factors using assessments and hiring steps.

To effectively utilize testing in your organization, your candidate assessment process should measure elements pulled from each of the following factors:

- Intelligence and cognitive ability

- Skill and vocational aptitude

- Reference checks from prior managers

- Personality profiling

Testing Intelligence and Cognitive Ability

Cognitive ability tests assess thinking abilities (e.g., reasoning, perception, memory, verbal and mathematical ability, and problem solving). Such tests pose questions designed to estimate an applicant's potential to use mental processes to solve work-related problems or acquire new job knowledge. A 2005 meta-analysis of the research on intelligence testing[14] found that tests of specific cognitive abilities are highly reliable and valid predictors of both job performance and training efficacy.

Researchers in this analysis looked at the difference in job performance between workers exhibiting high-cognitive ability and workers exhibiting lower measures of cognitive ability and found that the difference in scores could account for approximately 30 percent of the variance in job performance. These results mean that cognitive ability tests are typically the strongest predictor of job performance, beating out more popular evaluation techniques such as personality assessments and job interviews as stand-alone measures. Furthermore, the study showed that cognitive tests are useful predictors of success in most jobs in nearly all industries, although their ability to predict job performance is strongest for more complex roles, such as professional and managerial roles.

Incorporating an assessment that measures your candidates' cognitive ability will almost certainly lead to better hiring results.

Testing Skills

Skills tests can be conducted at any time in the interview process. They can be online or in person and be written or hands-on demonstrations

---

14   C. Bertua, N. Anderson, J. F. Salgado, "The predictive validity of cognitive ability tests: A UK meta-analysis," *Journal of Occupational and Organizational Psychology* 78 (2005): 387–409.

of a particular skill. The hard skills required for success in a job will vary from company to company and position to position, but the key to a successful skills test is consistency in how it is administered and evaluated.

Skill evaluation should be conducted in the initial stages of the screening process to validate the candidate's claims of skill proficiencies and save you the time of going further in the process with a candidate who lacks the requisite abilities. Why wait until after you've hired that new bookkeeper to realize that he doesn't have the skills to use the accounting system in place at your business? A properly administered test can measure proficiency with everything from specific software packages to mastery of the English language or the workings of an internal combustion engine.

The point here is that it's better to know *before* you waste time and money on an unqualified job prospect.

Effectively Using Personality Profiling

Although personality profiling is extremely helpful in guiding managers on the best way to onboard and manage a new hire, a personality profile should *never* be used as a basis for hiring or firing someone.

Four-quadrant personality assessments (also referred to as 4Q assessments) such as DiSC or Myers-Briggs (MBTI) classify the respondent as some combination of four different options labeled as letters, numbers, or colors. These assessments present candidates with a list of adjectives from which they select words that are the most or least like them to ultimately measure tendencies and preferences.

Personality assessments provide incredible value in applications like team-building, coaching, and cultural awareness, but have serious shortcomings when they are used to make hiring decisions. These tests are unreliable, inconsistent, and subjective. If you use a personality test in the hiring process, you may end up in court. For example, who's to say that someone with a direct communication style is going to make a better business development resource than someone who's more collaborative or more analytical? Do so-called extroverts make better accountants than their introverted peers? There's no meaningful link between personality type and job performance.

Personality profiling won't improve a hiring process. Managers use these tests for diagnosing onboarding and management effectiveness.

One of the most popular personality assessments used in the onboarding process is the DiSC Assessment. DiSC is a profiling tool that improves work productivity, teamwork, and communication by helping managers understand how their employees' work-style tendencies will fit with the manager's style and their new team's work dynamic.

For more information on skills and personality testing, visit www .hireology.com/testing.

Give Your Final Candidates a Homework Assignment

After conducting your final round of in-person interviews and scoring the results, you either have a clear front-runner candidate for the position, or have ruled out all candidates for the role and are beginning your search again from scratch. When you have a clear front-runner—or, even better, front-*runners*—it's time to see them in action. How? By giving them a homework assignment.

My recommendation is to give your finalist(s) a simple, straightforward assignment called the 30/60/90-day performance plan. This assignment will give you valuable insight into the approaches that your candidate will use to accomplish the necessary goals for their new role. To begin, we refer to the candidate scorecard, where all of these tasks have already been defined (another reason why completing the candidate scorecard is a must-do!).

At this stage, you'll likely have a few lingering questions or clarifications to make with your candidate from your previous interviews. Giving the 30/60/90-day homework assignment is the perfect opportunity to address these issues. You'll want to call your candidate to initiate the conversation. First, you'll give them feedback on their in-person interview. Second, you'll invite them in for a final, more informal conversation. Remember that this person is someone who will likely be working for you, and you're beginning the process of making a natural transition from candidate to employee. You want to set them up for success, and the psychological influence of this stage is immeasurable.

Invite your candidate back for a final conversation using the following telephone script.

Hi, [Candidate name], it's Adam from Acme Incorporated. I wanted to thank you for coming in the other day and spending time with us. Based on the past few weeks of conversations, I'm excited to say that we're confident that you're a good fit for this position, and I hope you feel that we're a good fit for you. Before we discuss an offer, I'd like to give you an opportunity to set your agenda for your first three months with us, and so I have a homework assignment for you. Based on your knowledge of the role, and of our company, I'd like for you to write a 30/60/90-day action plan for what you will do in the role over your first three months. I'm not looking for a detailed business plan or anything like that, but rather a bulleted list of the accomplishments you'd see as important to make in each of your first three months here. Once you're done with the plan we can get together and discuss it face-to-face. Do you think you could put something together for me by the end of the week?

Your candidate will ask some basic clarifying questions, so here is what you're looking for: A brief summary (one to two pages, tops) of actionable items that will be accomplished in 30, 60, and 90 days on the job. They should do the best they can with the information that they've been given. Tell them that your get-together at the end of the week will be an opportunity to discuss their plan and ensure that everyone is on the same page.

There are many benefits to this approach as you finalize your decision. If their plan indicates that their thinking and approach is aligned with yours and the organization, then you're in great shape. If, on the other hand, their proposals are way off base, it's time to reevaluate your choice. The most likely scenario is that you'll have an opportunity to clarify the priorities and list of must-dos, which is to everyone's benefit.

Consider the following as you prepare for this plan review meeting with your final candidate:

Time to Lighten Up

At this point, you're 90 percent sure that you've selected the right person for the job. This meeting is your opportunity to transition from interviewer and candidate to manager and employee. You're not offering the person the job yet, but it's time to shift from an interview mindset to a manager mindset. Make sure the dynamic of the interaction is supportive and collaborative. Because this person will likely be working for you in the near future, this meeting is the perfect chance for you to set the tone for their tenure with your organization.

Ask the Candidate to Present Their Plan

Here's how I typically start off the meeting:

"Hi, Julie, thanks for coming back in. I'm really excited to see what you've got in mind for your first ninety days on the job here."

Sit back and listen attentively. Don't coach the candidate—if they ask things like, "Should I stand?" or "Do you want a copy?" simply reply, "Do what you do!"

You are still evaluating this candidate's ability to perform in a high-pressure situation. It doesn't get much more high pressure than presenting your ideas to a potential boss with no safety net.

Notice the little things. They matter. Can this candidate deliver a good formal presentation? Are they clear and articulate? Do they project confidence in their plan? Do they qualify every goal before they give it (i.e., "I wasn't sure what you meant by, 'Grow sales by 30 percent in year one,' because I wasn't sure if you were referring to net new sales, or does that include upgrades from existing customers?"). Did they follow instructions? Are they off base with their assumptions? If so, did they bother to ask you for clarification prior to delivering their plan? Note all of these things.

Is the candidate's plan viable? Did their approach underwhelm you? Did they grossly overreach and deliver a plan that no one could achieve? Is their plan reasonable given the resources of the team and organization?

Don't interrupt the candidate. Let them finish without your influence biasing their delivery. At the conclusion of their presentation, ask specific questions about their plan. Question assumptions and provide corrections to any mistakes that you see. If you feel that the plan is too aggressive, say so. If you feel that the plan is too soft, say so. Finally, ensure that they can commit to this plan, because this plan will be used to evaluate their performance at a ninety-day review.

At the end of this presentation, you'll either confirm what you already know about this candidate, or you'll be hit with a left fielder that causes you to question your decision to make the hire. If you decide to move forward, you now have a ninety-day plan for managing this person's performance—written by the new employee! You'll take the guesswork out of your new employee's first ninety days and dramatically improve their chances of success. With this approach, it is impossible to have an employee that begins working without knowing what they're accountable for in their first three months. It's a powerful tool for managing new staff, and it creates a real sense of ownership and empowerment in your new hires.

Case Study: Get Interactive in Your Interviews

Nick Sarillo has carved quite a name for himself—and his pizza—amid one of the most competitive pizza markets: Chicago. But Sarillo, who owns two Nick's Pizza & Pub establishments, has perhaps made a bigger name for his progressive workplace culture. This culture has earned Sarillo's restaurants numerous awards for being one of the best places to work and accolades from publications like Inc. magazine. He's also helped coach other organizations on his famous "Trust and Track" management style.

The key to all that success, says Sarillo, who has also written *A Slice of the Pie*, a book that discusses his approach to creating a winning workforce culture, is to attract and retain great people.

"Nowadays everyone is having a hard time finding and keeping good people," says Sarillo. "But having a dynamic hiring program and culture attracts the best people. A great culture becomes a talent magnet."

Thanks to its culture, Nick's Pizza & Pub has become a cool place to get a job where demand often exceeds the supply of open positions. Even with more than two hundred employees, turnover is just 25 percent—about a third of the industry average, according to the National Restaurant Association.[15]

"The restaurant business is usually just a pass-through industry for most people," says Sarillo. "But at Nick's, it's a career opportunity. It's actually hard to get an interview with us."

So when a position opens up at one of Sarillo's establishments—a third location is in the works—it's a big deal that Sarillo takes seriously, regardless of what the position is.

Sarillo and his team's first priority is to identify candidates who match the purpose and values of his organization. He says they also look for qualities such as an ability to make eye contact and to connect with people rather than judging applicants on how much restaurant experience they have.

"We can track competencies and we can train the rest," says Sarillo. "I have outstanding employees who have never worked a day in a restaurant before they got here and they turned out to be amazing. Even our controller had never worked as an accountant before we hired him."

A key element of Sarillo's process for identifying high-potential candidates who will fit the company's culture is to take a team-based and interactive approach to interviewing. Every candidate's first interview is given by two of Nick's employees—and both employees question the candidate. In fact, any employee who is interested in getting trained on

---

15   "Employee turnover rate tops 70% in 2015," National Restaurant Association, March 22, 2016, http://www.restaurant.org/News-Research/News/ Employee-turnover-rate-tops-70-in-2015.

how to hire is given two days of interview training to help make sure everyone is working off the same script.

"We are teaching employees how to track the nuances of language and energy and ask the questions that allow you to go deeper," says Sarillo. "Our goal is to hit the bull's-eye and not just the target with our interviews."

All interviews are conducted in a circle, with no table or chair between the candidate and the interviewers. This way, the interviewers can watch a candidate's body language as they answer challenging questions such as, "Tell me about a time you saw someone stealing. What did you do?"

"We can track how they handle that stressful conversation," says Sarillo. "Does their complexion change? Do their ears turn red? Do they shift in their seat? These are all things that can be hard to learn if you don't interview someone in person."

Interviews at Nick's are also interactive, especially when it comes to assessing if there is a performance match between the company and the candidate.

"We want to run through an exercise to make sure their idea of hard work or what a clean table looks like matches with our expectation," says Sarillo.

If the person is applying for a server position, for example, Sarillo might have the person suggest two appetizers from the menu. If the person is applying for a hostess position, he might ask them to answer the phone as if a live customer were on the other end. After the exercise is complete, Sarillo might ask the candidate to assess how they thought they performed on a scale of one to five. The interviewers would also rate the candidate's performance and then compare the results to see how self-aware the candidate was—and whether there is a potential match or not.

"If they give themselves a five and we gave them a one, we can stop right there because that's a no hire," says Sarillo.

Sarillo is also a proponent of asking open-ended questions that dig deeper into the candidate's motivations and encourage them to explain themselves better.

"We ask follow-ups like 'Why did you do that?' or 'How did you do that?' or 'Give us one more example,' as a way to get to the core of that person," he says.

When it comes to assessing whether someone fits within the organization's values, Sarillo says he doesn't ask if someone agrees with those values. Rather, he'll ask a candidate how they have lived out a particular value recently in their own lives. One of the values at Nick's is ongoing learning and development. A question Sarillo might ask a candidate would be, "What in the past six months have you done to develop yourself?"

At the same time, Sarillo tries to be as efficient as possible with the time he and his team spend on interviews. If he notices that a candidate tends to take a long time answering questions, for instance, he might challenge that person to give their answer in a single sentence.

Sarillo also tells candidates right up front that he won't answer any questions during the interview until the end.

"An interviewee will [commonly] ask a lot of questions and when [the interviewer] loves their [personality], [the interviewer] will spend the entire interview giving away all the answers," says Sarillo. "We ask people to hold their questions until we are done. We then learn a lot based on the questions they do or don't ask us."

After the candidate leaves their first interview, the two interviewers compare notes on how the candidate scored relative to performance and cultural fit. If there are more pluses than negatives from both interviewers, than the candidate gets a second interview (management level positions also need to pass a third interview). If there is disagreement between the two sets of scores, it becomes an opportunity for the interviewers to talk through the differences and check whether someone missed something the other person picked up on.

"There is real value in having a second perspective to compare with," says Sarillo.

Nick's also has a strong onboarding program to shepherd new employees into the company's culture and to help them live the brand promise by feeling accepted, supported, and set up for success.

● ● ●

CHAPTER SUMMARY

Most managers make the mistake of having casual conversations during interviews with candidates instead of coming prepared with specific questions. They also talk more than the candidate does, wasting time. To conduct an effective in-person interview, you need to be prepared not just with specific questions, but willingness to ask follow-ups. You only get a sense of whether or not the candidate you are interviewing is a good fit for the position by digging deep.

Managers also often miss the opportunity to give candidates a sense of what their job will look like once they start and the expectations to which they'll be held. This lack of clarity leads to a sense of broken promises and can produce higher than expected turnover. You can avoid these missteps by giving your candidate a homework assignment that doubles as an onboarding plan. Unqualified candidates will typically opt out before you go any further.

SELF-ANALYSIS

Ask yourself the following questions:

- Think back to your last interview; was it a conversation where you talked more than the candidate?

- How do you prepare for an interview?

- How do you talk to new hires about what will be expected of them during the first few months on the job?

KEY TAKEAWAYS

By rethinking your approach to interviews, you can more effectively screen out people who fit your organization from those who don't.

1 Create a game plan that you can use for every interview; don't wing it. This way when you evaluate candidates you know you are comparing apples to apples.

2 Use testing and assessments to determine how your candidates will fit inside your organization.

3 Give your candidate a chance to map out their first few months on the job. This assignment will create shared expectations about what the job will entail. You'll also develop trust and an objective mechanism to evaluate the candidate.

Chapter Seven

TRUST BUT VERIFY

You've put your top candidates through the interview gauntlet. You've liked what you've heard. The Super Elements are in place. The candidate's work history seems legit and you were impressed with their 30/60/90-day plan. It's time to make them an offer, right? Not quite. Double-check everything they told you.

Begin with performing a reference check, a step that surprisingly the majority of entrepreneurs and business managers fail to complete during their hiring process. If you're sitting there reading this and you are one of those managers who never conducts reference checks, I want you to throw some cold water on your face and promise, "I will never fail to conduct reference checks again."

Would you ever consider forking over $400,000 for a house based entirely on what the selling agent told you? ("Of *course* the house is mold-free!") Not a chance; that's what home inspections are for. Yet, almost every entrepreneur I work with is willing to fork over $50,000, $80,000, or $100,000 a year (or more) for someone they're hiring based entirely on the belief that this person hasn't embellished or inflated a *single thing* about their accomplishments or experience. Faith in people is a good thing, but when you're hiring new employees you should "trust but verify."

As much as we'd like to believe everything that candidates tell us, it's the reference check that tells us whether or not the results that they *said* they achieved ever actually existed. If you rely solely on the candidate's word, you're guaranteed to make hires that result in missed expectations. Until you ask the candidate's former supervisors a few critical questions, you can't be sure that you know what you're getting.

Guidelines for a Successful Reference Check

Most managers who conduct reference checks blow through the call in about five minutes. "What can you tell me about Jim? Any performance issues? Well, great! Talk to you later."

A good rule of thumb is that hiring the wrong person costs you ten times that person's base salary after you factor in compensation, benefits, lost customer opportunities, and other opportunity costs. Let's say you're hiring a $50,000-a-year resource for your growing company. You're making a $500,000 buying decision. Even when you're hiring a seemingly inexpensive resource, act like it's a half-million dollar decision. It is.

The reference check is the most important part of the interview process, because it's the first time that you have someone other than your candidate talking about that candidate's performance. Don't rush through this final screening step!

Here are a few simple guidelines to follow when conducting a reference check on your top candidate:

Reference Checks Should Be Conducted by the Hiring Manager

That's you. This is your opportunity to talk to a fellow manager who has direct experience working with the person you're planning to hire. You're going to get extremely relevant information and a keen sense whether or not the candidate performed as advertised. When you pawn off reference checks onto your HR manager, you're robbing yourself of one of the most accurate predictors of this candidate's success in your role.

Reference Checks Should Be Performed after the Final Interview

Reference checks are the last step in the process for a reason. Don't waste your time conducting reference checks for candidates who haven't made the final cut yet. After your final interviews, if you have two candidates of equal merit, it's the reference checks that will tell you whom to hire.

Coworkers Are Not Real References

Candidates will often provide names of people who were really coworkers, or managers that didn't directly supervise the candidate. I'll talk to these people, but I want to speak with the candidate's direct supervisor for every job that they've had over the last five to ten years. Great candidates keep in touch with their managers and have no problem connecting you with them. Mediocre candidates tend to lose touch with their previous managers and will reluctantly track them down when asked to do so. Bad candidates will tell you that their manager is no longer with that company and that the last time they checked, the person had moved to Sri Lanka. If a candidate is unwilling to connect you with their former supervisor, it should be an automatic disqualification.

Ask the Candidate to Set Up the Reference Call

The candidate should contact their references and schedule your calls for the evening or weekend. This approach accomplishes two things. First, it puts the reference at ease because the candidate has asked them to speak with you. When the reference feels like they have the candidate's permission to talk to you, they'll give you great information.

Second, it frees up the reference from the constraints of talking to you during business hours. Many companies have policies that forbid their managers from giving references during business hours, if at all. Asking them to speak to you on off-hours will put most managers at ease.

When you talk to the references, pay attention if a manager tells you they're unable to give information beyond verifying the candidate's employment dates. What are they afraid of telling you? People are typically more than happy to give glowing references for great people who once worked for them. Poor performers? Not so much. Make sure you tell the references you contact that the call will be confidential.

Reference checks are a must-do. Discipline yourself to spend the extra hour or two making these calls yourself, and watch your hiring results improve immediately.

Conducting a Reference Check

A reference check phone call should take no more than twenty minutes, barring some unforeseen revelation that merits a deeper dive. If you're running longer than twenty minutes, you risk annoying the reference who was nice enough to take your call. The following approach is designed to put the reference at ease and slowly progress to more probing questions:

Talk to the Reference as a Peer

For example, your call might go something like:

"Hi, Jon, this is Adam Robinson from ABC Motors, calling in reference to Stephanie Smith. Stephanie told me that this would be a good time to speak with you. Thanks for taking my call. Jon, I'm in charge of sales hiring here, and Stephanie is being considered for a sales position with our company that's similar to the role she had with you. As a fellow manager who had the opportunity to work with Stephanie, I was hoping that you could give me some insights into her job performance while she worked for you, and that this call will help me better manage her if we decide to add her to the team. I promise that the contents of our conversation will remain between us. I just want to know your thoughts so I make a more informed decision."

Clue In to the Nuances of the Reference's Responses

Some answers to the reference check are buried in the subtleties of the reference's voice inflection and tone. Does it sound like the reference is holding back about something negative? Are you getting stonewalled on your questions? Just scratching the surface? Getting nothing more than one-word answers? If you think any of these scenarios are the case, simply say, "Tell me more about that."

Push the reference to give you the second, third, and even fourth layer of detail. These layers are where the reality of your candidate's performance history lives.

During these calls, it is essential to *take notes.* Write down everything you hear, good and bad. If you don't, you'll forget half the stuff that you're told within five minutes of hanging up the phone.

When it comes to what you should be asking during the reference check calls, ask the following questions, in order:

1 Let me tell you about the job I am considering hiring [candidate] for. [Describe job]. Based on your experience with [candidate], how do you think they might perform in this role?

Answers here will range from, "Oh, that's a perfect job for them" to "You know, I'm not really sure because here they did something that was different."

No matter the answer, we're going to probe for specifics. If you're getting the feeling that your role is likely a stretch, ask the reference, "Do you think that this role is a stretch for them?"

If the answer is anything other than, "No, they'll do fine" you'll want to pause.

2 "Let's talk about their job while working for you. What were [candidate's] responsibilities when they worked for you?" (Follow-up question: "What metrics did you use to measure their performance?")

The answers to this question will tell you whether or not your candidate embellished their job responsibilities. I can't tell you how many times I've asked a reference this question only to realize that my candidate never had any real supervisory duties but simply worked as a senior member of a sales team, or some similar example. Candidates love to overdescribe their duties, but here's where we find out the truth.

3 "When it comes to [candidate], what really stands out from a performance standpoint?"

Listen intently, and ask follow-up questions. Statements like "tell me more about that" will elicit a deeper response than simply letting the reference run through the list without pausing to elaborate. Make sure you walk away from this question understanding this person's opinion of your candidate's strengths.

4 "What would you consider to be [the candidate's] biggest areas for improvement?"

This question yields huge insight. Do they tell you, "They didn't really have any weaknesses"? If so, they were probably not an effective manager and therefore the reference should be eyed suspiciously. Does the reference go into specific detail without being prompted? If so, that's the sign of a great manager-employee relationship (their trust was strong). After your reference concludes their initial list, be sure to pinpoint each item with a follow-up question like, "Tell me more about [trait] that you just described."

5 "On a scale of one to ten, with ten being 'outstanding,' how would you rate [candidate's] overall performance?"

As always, probe for specifics reasons for the rating given. Anything less than a grade of eight should raise alarm bells in your head. Make sure to dig into the specifics. Anything less than a seven is a bad omen.

6 "When did [candidate] work for you?" "Can you confirm for me how [candidate]'s compensation was structured?"

These answers are typically straightforward. Here we're making sure that what the candidate told us about their job tenure and compensation and what the reference tells us match up. It's another place where discrepancies will abound, and typical issues involve the candidate's stating their total compensation potential as higher than it actually was. When candidates inflate compensation, the most common method is to state that they had larger potential bonuses or incentives than was the case.

7 "Is there anything that you've observed about your time managing [candidate] that I should be aware of, good or bad?"

Listen and learn. Probe for specifics when your instincts tell you to do so.

8 "What's the best advice you can give me about how I can best manage [candidate]?"

The answer to this question is many times the most telling answer of all. Read between the lines and you'll often uncover emotions ranging from "you really have to stay on top of things with them" (bad) to something like "I sure wish they still worked here" (good).

9 "Is there anything else about [candidate] that you feel is important for my overall evaluation of their fit for my open position?"

You'll usually get a repeat of a previous answer—or some flavor of it—that is innocuous more often than not. Occasionally, you'll get some new info . . . which is why we ask this question.

10 "I'd like to thank you for your time today. May I ask you one final question? If given the opportunity to hire [candidate] again for a similar job, would you do so enthusiastically?"

Any answer other than some version of "absolutely!" is the manager more likely than not telling you that hiring this person will lead to issues. If it sounds like this person would be even the least bit hesitant to rehire your candidate, take heed. If they qualify their answer, take heed. It's for a reason. Seek clarification, but don't try to convince yourself that you should hire someone whom you know is getting a lukewarm rehire reception from a former manager. If the answer is no, I would not recommend a single circumstance when hiring the person anyway is worth the risk. I mean, this reference just told you that they wouldn't choose to hire your candidate. What more info do you need?

This ten-question reference check format works exceptionally well for most positions. Use it with confidence.

Conducting Background Checks

Let's say you've just hired a controller for your business. You're giving this person responsibility over your company's entire financial operation—cash management, banking, client receivables—the whole enchilada. You're excited because you're finally freeing yourself up to focus on other things that you need to grow your business.

The problem is, your new controller is facing personal bankruptcy. As a matter of fact, this new dream hire is struggling under a mountain of credit card debt. His minimum monthly payments are taking up over 60 percent of his personal income. Debt collectors have filed liens against his house for unpaid bills, and credit card companies have flagged his account for multiple late payments and defaults.

Now, two questions: First, wouldn't you want to know these things *before* you put this guy on the corporate checking account? Second, why didn't you find this out until after you realized that he'd stolen over $450,000 from under your nose?

You read about these stories all the time, cases where a newly hired controller single-handedly pilfers almost half a million dollars without anyone having the slightest clue about what they were doing. Not only did this person have access to the company checkbook, but they were also responsible for booking the accounting entries and performing the bank reconciliations—a sure-fire recipe for fraud. The new hire simply set up a few fictitious companies and started sending himself checks. You hear stories like this all the time, where it took two years to find out what happened until after the company bounced a payroll run.

"I couldn't believe it," the CEO always gets quoted as saying. "Here I am, a trustworthy person, assuming that everyone is as trustworthy as me. I nearly lost my business."

The case for conducting credit, drug, and background checks is clear and compelling. You can never be too careful when hiring new employees. Our increasingly networked world makes it easier and easier for unscrupulous employees to siphon off thousands of dollars without you having a clue until it's too late.

Yes, conducting these necessary background checks requires a bit of additional time and money. Yes, it involves an extra step in the hiring process. But so what? Are you really prepared to take a massive financial hit because you're too busy to worry about properly vetting your employees? Unless your state prohibits the use of criminal background checks as a basis for turning down an application for employment, use them (but consult your labor attorney first!).

You need to understand that the employees who can cause you significant harm do not look like criminals, whatever that means. You can't pick them out from the crowd. One of the only ways you'll identify them is by conducting thorough background checks.

Once you've set up a proper credit, drug, and background check program, you're back in control of your decision making. Never hire someone without putting them through this process. It's not worth it to cut corners.

CHAPTER SUMMARY

No matter how rigorous the interview process has been, you still need to put in the extra effort to verify everything you have heard from your top candidates. Failing to contact references or conduct a background check is like buying a house without first having it inspected. It's just too risky. Fortunately, there are established and objective guidelines you should follow when it comes to verifying your top candidate's credentials. It takes more time, but avoiding a bad hire is an enormous payoff. In other words: trust, but verify.

SELF-ANALYSIS

Ask yourself the following questions:

- Do you employ reference checks as part of your hiring process? Why or why not?

- Can you think of a scenario where conducting a reference check would have helped you avoid a bad hire?

- What are some things you'd love to know about a candidate from their former boss or colleague?

KEY TAKEAWAYS

1 Implementing a formal reference and background check is not an option; it will greatly decrease your chances of a bad hire.

2 Creating a repeatable reference and background check process may reduce the risk related to charges of bias or discrimination.

3 Vetting your top candidates properly will help you sleep better at night. Trust but verify.

Chapter Eight

MAKE AN OFFER THEY CAN'T REFUSE

You started with fifteen telephone interviews, then invited five finalists in for personal interviews. You then narrowed the five final candidates down to the one candidate you feel is the best person for the job. The reference check and background check both came back stellar. You've had the candidate complete a homework assignment to show their chops. Now you're ready to offer your final candidate the job!

A lot of managers stumble in the job offer stage. The offer stage of the hiring process is similar to the closing stage of a sales process. If the salesperson has been consistently uncovering facts, exploring buyer motivation, understanding the hot-button issues, and trial closing their prospect along the way, then the sales process won't run off the road and into a ditch. However, if the salesperson has failed to uncover and handle the multiple objections that lie beneath the surface of every prospect's buying decision, then the prospect may end up saying, "You know, we've decided to go with another supplier." It's a terrible outcome, and the same thing can happen to your top recruits.

You can avoid those situations. There are a few basic guidelines to follow that will make for smooth sailing during the offer stage:

Know the Hot Button Issues

How far will your candidate have to commute to get to your job? Does this candidate want to work from home whenever they feel like it? Will this candidate balk at overnight travel? What about weekend travel? What benefits—health insurance, dental coverage, 401(k) match—are most important to this candidate? What mix of base and incentive compensation is acceptable to your candidate? If you haven't uncovered the answers to these and other basic questions, then you're setting yourself up for a surprise rejection.

Know Where You Stand

Does this candidate have other job offers pending? Other interviews scheduled? Where does your job opportunity stand in relation to the candidate's other options? Don't wait until you get a rejected job opportunity to realize that your top candidate had your job ranked as their backup option.

Use Verbal Trial Closes to Keep the Process Moving

The *trial close* is a sales tactic that feels out a prospect at various stages prior to the actual closing conversation. Good recruiters use trial closes to feel out their candidates after each step of the recruiting process.

"Nancy, let's say that we get through this process and agree that this is a great mutual fit. Assuming a base salary of X, with on-target earnings of Y, and a benefits package of Z, is this a position that you would feel comfortable accepting?"

The key here is to probe for specifics, no matter the answer. If there is any hesitation on your candidate's part, there's something you don't know. Find out.

Issue the Offer Verbally before Issuing a Written Offer

Do *not* email an offer to a candidate and have it be the first time they're reviewing numbers and terms. When you're ready to issue an offer, call the candidate. Once you get them on the phone, tell them you're pleased to inform them that they've been selected for the position. Thank them for their persistence through this lengthy but thorough process. Tell them that you'd like to take a moment to walk them through the offer verbally before sending the formal offer to them. After you've walked through the offer, ask them if they have any questions. Answer them. Ask them if they have any issues or concerns. Address them. If you feel like there are any loose ends, do *not* make the written offer. You have no idea whether or not this person is going to accept it. Wait until you have addressed all issues to the candidate's satisfaction, and *then* send the written offer. Otherwise, it's akin to a salesperson sending over a proposal via email and hoping the prospect says yes.

Use a Standard Offer Template

Don't re-create an offer letter from scratch every time you hire someone. A good offer letter is as much a marketing document as it is a statement of facts. Is it readable? Does it have a professional appearance? Does it touch on the major points? Additionally, your standard offer template should set a time certain when the offer expires. It should also tell the candidate to sign and email the offer letter back to you by a certain time (72 hours is my standard recommendation) to indicate their acceptance of your job offer. Do not make an open-ended offer, because you'll lose the ability to dictate tempo. If the candidate asks for an extension, ask them why. Many candidates asking for an extension on an offer decision do so because they're waiting for another job offer to come through. That's okay, but you definitely want to know that. Another reason candidates ask for an extension is that they want to talk it over with their spouse. You should rarely, if ever, grant extensions longer than a week.

Follow these straightforward guidelines to improve your offer acceptance rates.

How to Issue a Written Job Offer

The final step in the hiring process is the issuance of a written job offer. By the time you reach this step, you've reached a near-certainty that you've selected the right person for the job, and, if you've been following my advice on issuing verbal job offers prior to written ones, then you've already received a verbal acceptance from your candidate.

The only goal here is to prevent a last-minute surprise—and, at this point, the only thing you can do wrong is to accidentally omit essential information from the offer letter. To ensure that you cover everything you need, I'll run through the elements of a well-crafted job offer with you here. Feel free to use these guidelines as a template for your company's offer letter. *[Note: This document is in no way to be construed as legal advice. Please consult a labor attorney prior to issuing any formal job offers.]*

These are the major elements of the written job offer:

The Introduction

Here, we'll include all pertinent information about the job title, start date, and a disclosure that nothing is final until all due diligence has been completed (you always want an out, just in case!).

The Tangibles

The contents of this section will vary widely, depending on your company's compensation and benefits structure. I have included the most commonly used elements for this template.

The Legal Notice

In this section, you will remind them that employment is at-will and that this offer supersedes any prior discussion of compensation or benefits. *[Note: Not all states in the US are at-will employment states. Consult an attorney. Seriously.]*

The Conclusion

You can get as mushy with this as you'd like. I prefer to keep it simple.

Dear [first name],

I am pleased to offer you the position of [position title] with [company name]. Your anticipated start date is [month, day, year] and is contingent upon successful completion of the required credit and background check, the completion of our reference checking process, and acceptance of our standard confidentiality/non-compete agreement.

Your compensation will be the following:

Base Salary: $[amount] annualized, paid [bi-weekly/semi-monthly/ etc.].

Performance-based compensation: 20 percent of base salary, or $23,388, earned within the guidelines of the [company name] Incentive Compensation plan.

Bonus Potential: Discretionary, based on achievement of the company's operating goals and your individual performance.

Employee Stock Options: Participation in the [company name] Employee Stock Option program, at an initial grant of [number] option units.

Performance Review: Performance reviews are conducted twice annually, once in June and once in December. Raises in base salary are considered on an annual basis.

Paid Time Off (PTO): You will be eligible for [number] days PTO during each 12-month period.

Sick/Personal Days: [number] days for use during each 12-month period, beginning on your [number] day of employment.

Benefits: As a full-time employee, you will be eligible for our standard benefits plan, which includes Medical, Dental, Vision, Long-Term and Short-Term Disability, and Life Insurance. 401(k) eligibility begins after [# months, years, etc.] of continuous employment.

Employment with [company name] is considered at-will. Either party is free to terminate the employment relationship with or without cause or notice. This offer letter supersedes all other oral and/or written agreements.

This offer is valid through [5 days from date of issue]. Upon acceptance of this offer, please sign below and return this letter to my attention via email at [email address]. I will also send you a new hire packet for you to complete and bring with you on your start date. If you have any questions regarding our offer, please call me at (###) ###-####.

We look forward to working with you!

Sincerely, AGREED AND ACCEPTED:

[hiring manager] _____

[title] [Name] [Date]

That's it. All done.

Once you've completed your offer, send a copy to your candidate via email and ask them to sign and scan a copy back to you. Once you receive their signed offer, make sure you have two originals to sign once they come in for the onboarding discussion.

Congratulations! You just added a new member to the team.

Preventing Last-Minute Surprises in Recruiting

You talked to the candidate on Friday, and they verbally accepted the position.

"That all sounds great," they said after hearing your verbal offer. "I look forward to reviewing your offer over the weekend."

You're thrilled, because you've *finally* filled the most important open position in your company.

Then comes Monday. Your phone rings. It's your dream candidate on the other end of the line. "Hi. You know, after talking over the offer with my family, I'm unfortunately going to have to decline."

You ask why. The candidate gives you some song and dance about this decision being best for their family. You're stunned—on Friday, everything was great. What the heck just happened?

When you get served with a healthy dose of Monday morning surprise, it means that you've failed to close your candidate before giving them the job offer. It happens to everyone, but it doesn't have to happen often. So, how do you avoid getting slammed with a last-minute offer rejection? To answer that question, let's take a look at the most common reasons that candidates do a 180 on your job offer:

The Spouse

Spouses are the leading cause of death for job offers. When I was a full-time executive recruiter, the most common reason cited for last-minute offer declines was, "I talked it over with my husband/wife."

I remember one instance when the candidate wanted to take the job, but her husband was skeptical about the viability of the company. I ended up on the phone with the candidate for almost two hours. There *is* a better way to approach this problem. Simply ask your candidate, "Have you talked about this job opportunity with your family?" during the "verbal acceptance" phone call. If they say no, you have a problem. If they say yes, ask them what their family thought about their decision to explore other career possibilities. Act on the answer accordingly.

The Pay

Don't put yourself in the situation when the first time you discuss money with the candidate is in the job offer, because you're setting yourself up for disaster. Ask for the candidate's minimum acceptable compensation on the job application. Why waste your time with someone who wants $30,000 a year more than you're able to spend?

The Bennies

In today's environment, great health insurance and perks like a 401(k) match are huge factors in a candidate's career choices. The best talent will work for employers who offer the broadest range of goodies. Make sure you understand which benefits are must-haves for your candidate. How? Ask them, "What benefits are must-haves for you? Any deal-breakers?"

They'll tell you what they expect, and you'll avoid that awkward moment when the candidate tells you, "I don't see tuition reimbursement on the offer letter."

If you don't offer tuition reimbursement, and your candidate has another offer from a company who does, and it's a hot button issue for them—good-bye, candidate.

The Other Company

Sometimes candidates have preferences that transcend basic compensation and benefits. Maybe they'll take a huge pay cut to work for Google. Maybe they've decided that *any* offer from company X is better than your best offer. The point is, sometimes it doesn't matter what you offer—if a person has decided that company X is their end-all and be-all employer, your offer is in bad shape. Wouldn't you like to know this information up front? That's why I ask the candidate, "What other job options are you taking a look at? How does our job rank in relation to the others? If Company X made you an offer that was identical to ours, which one would you take?"

I ask those questions *during the phone screen.*

These are some common sources of last-minute surprises. Now that you know how to uncover these common landmines, you can avoid them and make offers to candidates that have a high acceptance rate.

Case Study: Avoid Surprises When You're Hiring

As a serial tech entrepreneur, Ajay Goel knows how difficult it can be to find and keep top talent. In his years of running JangoMail, which he founded in 2002 and later sold in 2013, and, more recently, Wordzen, an email writing service he started in 2015, Goel says he has learned a few key lessons in building his teams.

One of the things he learned was to not overpay anyone so that they would come work for him—especially people with high-demand skills like software developers. Not only could he not afford to compete against the salaries of tech giants in Silicon Valley, Goel learned that extending someone a big paycheck was no guarantee that the hire would stick around for enough time to justify all the up-front investment needed to bring them on board.

What did work, however, was offering the kind of culture and work environment that developers could see themselves thriving in—which included lots of autonomy and recognition for hard work and accomplishments.

Goel also recognized that a key part of building a great and sustainable team was doing a better job at avoiding surprises during his hiring process.

Goel never turned to recruiters to find talent. He relied instead on placing ads on Craigslist in markets outside of the big tech meccas. Those ads also contained a homework assignment that sharp candidates would have no problem solving and discussing in their cover letters when they applied for the position.

"I rarely read a resume," says Goel. "The most important factors for me during the initial screen were the cover letters and how the candidates solved the problem. It might only have taken them ten to fifteen minutes to solve it, but I wanted to see if they put in that effort."

Another key step that Goel adopted in his hiring process was incorporating more substantial reference checks. In the beginning, he admits he was doing it all wrong by only talking to people that the candidate provided contact information for. After realizing he wasn't getting much value out of those conversations, Goel changed his approach to reference checks. He started asking the candidate to provide the names of their last three supervisors and to introduce Goel to each of them in an email. This email also asks the supervisors when they could set up a thirty- to sixty-minute phone call with Goel to discuss the candidate.

"This way you put the burden of the introduction on the candidate," says Goel. "You're in control and they aren't dictating who you are speaking to."

Goel says that changing his approach to reference checks had a big influence on several of his hiring decisions. Sometimes, he felt good about hiring a candidate until talking to their references. He gained insight into elements like whether someone met deadlines or showed up to work when they were supposed to—things only a supervisor could tell you.

"I would have otherwise hired that person and had a fail," he says.

"You need to be on alert for surprises at all times when you're hiring, even when you're ready to extend an offer to a candidate," says Goel. He remembers one experience when he was ready to hire a server administrator. The candidate was someone ready to make the jump from a larger established retailer to a start-up. The candidate was attracted by the idea of working for a fast-growing company, even if it meant giving up some of the stability and benefits his current employer was able to offer.

Goel was excited to bring the candidate on, so he made him an offer he knew would be attractive based on their conversations. But then— nothing. The candidate decided not to take the job. Goel was floored. What had gone wrong?

Eventually, Goel learned that the candidate's spouse was not as on board with the career shift as her husband was and she effectively nixed his taking the job. "The lesson learned," says Goel, "is to make sure you ask a candidate about how their significant other feels about the opportunity during the interview process."

"You need to have both people on board to make it work," says Goel. "If they aren't, or there is any hesitation, you need to address it. Otherwise it becomes a waste of everyone's time to go any further."

● ● ●

CHAPTER SUMMARY

The final step in the hiring process is making the candidate you want an offer they can't refuse. By using a formalized and repeatable process, you'll help ensure that you address any concerns your top candidates might have while also ensuring that you are setting mutual expectations and building trust. A formalized process will also help you avoid last-minute surprises that might result in losing a top candidate.

SELF-ANALYSIS

Ask yourself the following questions:

- Have you ever had the perfect candidate walk away at the last minute? Why did that happen?

- What kinds of questions do you ask to make sure the candidate wants the job you are offering?

- Do you address any concerns a candidate's spouse or significant other might have before you extend them an offer?

KEY TAKEAWAYS

1 Formalize the process of extending an offer to your top candidates; it will you help ensure they take your offer.

2 Ask the candidate about extenuating circumstances before you extend them an offer, such as objections from their spouse or significant other, or other job offers they have pending. Asking will help you avoid disappointment and drama.

3 Confirm the job offer verbally with your candidate before you make a written offer. When you let your candidate know how much you want them onboard, make sure the feeling is mutual.

RETAIN YOUR BEST

Chapter Nine

START OFF ON THE RIGHT FOOT

Your work doesn't stop once you've made the decision to hire someone. If you want to retain them over the long run and build a great team, you need to have a solid plan to onboard your people.

"The hiring process doesn't end when someone joins the team," says William Tincup.

The hiring process extends through the onboarding process, at least ninety days after the new employee's first day. The onboarding process is not just an opportunity to sign insurance forms and review the employee handbook. It is a time when the organization and the candidate decide whether they made the right choice.

"We have to keep checking in with the new hire to find out what's holding them back from being successful," says Tincup. "We need to find out what we need to start doing, and stop doing, to help them. You need to ask those questions. That's how you show people that you care about their success and not just recruiting them."

Onboarding is the process of agreeing to expectations between you and your new employee, a mutual promise as to what you as an employer expect in terms of performance and what your new team member can expect from you. If you don't have a well-structured onboarding process, you open yourself up to surprises and frustrated expectations. Great people leave their jobs when promises aren't met.

When was the last time you hired someone and were frustrated by that new employee's performance after just three months? Or, was there a time you lost a great employee after they told you that the job wasn't anything like they thought it would be? Both of these cases could have been avoided by holding a conversation up front that set mutual expectations for the employee and the manager. An effective onboarding process results in shared expectations and a shared commitment to meet those expectations between the employee and the employer.

The onboarding process starts by introducing the new employee to their team. Then you need to explain how the employee's job directly relates to the mission, vision, and values of your organization.

Discovering Your Core Values

Authentic culture is easy to spot: You can *feel* it. It's inescapable, invigorating, and infectious to those who are a part of it. Vendors arrive for meetings and leave feeling like they want to quit their job and come work there. People absolutely love what they're doing, and you get the sense that most people would do just about anything to help their teammate or their company achieve success.

Manufactured culture is easy to spot, too: You'll see all the accoutrements of a great culture but feel none of the energy. There's the *de riguer* open-layout office design, but nobody is talking to one another. No one is smiling, and you'll watch people take their plate of catered food and go back to their desk and eat it while reading social media updates with their headphones on. There's a foosball table nobody uses, because managers shoot dirty looks to the employees when they use it. The leadership sends incredulous emails to one another saying they can't believe the office is empty at 5:15 p.m. every day.

An authentic culture starts with authentic core values. What's a *core value*? It's a statement that declares something your company believes, one facet of the way your company chooses to conduct itself. A core value is non-negotiable, and it never changes. It's an invisible hand, guiding every decision that every person (yes, including you) makes in the organization.

Core values can lack authenticity. Does your management team let employees slide on delivering what they promised? If yes, don't say that "accountability" is a core value. Are you giving your customers a refund every time one is requested, regardless of the reason? If you're not, don't say that "the customer is always right," because your decisions don't reflect that particular value. Does your management team *really* trust employees to get the job done, no matter what, regardless of the time of day the work is being performed? If the real answer is no, don't buy the foosball table. Everyone will see that it makes you angry when people are playing it at 2:15 p.m. on a Tuesday, and it will become a visible symbol of your inauthentic culture.

Are you willing to fire a top performer for violating a core value of your company? If the answer is no, it's not a core value; it's a statement that someone thought sounded good but nobody really believes. This dissonance will erode the *esprit de corps* of your organization, and lead to consistent underperformance.

Core values are the essential ingredient for a great culture. How, then, do you communicate your company's core values to a new employee? You do it in the onboarding process. There are four key topics you need to cover when you talk to your new employee about how their job fits in the big picture:

1. Communicate and Teach Your Core Values

The onboarding process is your best opportunity to share with your new employee what values the organization lives by, and to do so in a way that is easily understood and implementable. These are the guidelines you evaluate and recognize performance with throughout the organization. Ideally, your values are reinforced quarterly, monthly, and even daily by calling out people—especially through peer-to-peer nominations—who truly live your core values as they do their work.

It can also be valuable to share your organization's *anti-values*, or the behaviors and attitudes that are the opposite of how you want to live.

At Hireology, our core values are:

Pathological Optimism

Building a successful business from scratch requires a level of perseverance and drive that few possess. The odds are completely stacked against us: There will always be a better-funded or larger competitor; there will always be a process that's broken or something that could be done more efficiently. We accept this reality, and we focus on winning.

Anti-value: *Constant negativity or pessimism*

Own the Result

If we're going to succeed, we have to be accountable for the promises we make to ourselves, our fellow Hireologists, and our customers. Ownership of the results that each of us produce—good or bad—is ours. We thank our teammates for their contributions to our company's success, but we look to ourselves when things come up short. This is an awesome place to work for people who value accountability.

Anti-value: *Assigning blame*

Create Wow Moments

We live in a world of low expectations and mediocrity, so we strive to exceed expectations for our customers and our teammates whenever possible. Hireologists know that a little extra effort goes a long way. We take the time to do the unexpected, because that's how we build strong relationships and create raving fans.

Anti-value: *Doing the minimum required*

Eager to Improve

There's not a person here who can claim to know everything there is to know about their job. We're all learning, and Hireologists aren't afraid of feedback from our customers or teammates that helps them grow. We open our minds, drop the defensiveness, and actively seek out feedback because it energizes us. People who don't like hearing constructive feedback aren't going to like working here.

Anti-value: *I know better than you do*

No Assholes

We treat our teammates and our customers with trust and respect. There's zero tolerance at Hireology for disrespectful behavior, both to our teammates and to our customers. Hireologists and customers who violate this core value aren't around for long.

Anti-value: *Being an asshole*

2. Describe the Organization's Mission and Vision

Once you have covered what your organization's values are, you have the opportunity to discuss with your new employee the reason why your organization exists: What is the purpose, cause, or passion that everyone is reaching for collectively?

Here are a few great examples of company mission:

Mary Kay Cosmetics: To give unlimited opportunity to women.

Disney: To make people happy.

Nike: To help people experience the emotion of competition, winning, and beating competitors.

If a *mission* is defined as your purpose, passion, or cause, then what is your *vision*? Your company vision is the answer to this simple question: What does your organization do better than anyone else out there?

A few great examples of company vision:

Walgreens: To have the most convenient drugstores in the best locations.

Facebook: To connect the world.

Amazon: To allow anyone to find and buy anything they want online.

Your goal here is to craft a story that imparts these important concepts—mission and vision—to your new hire in a way that makes the concepts real and meaningful. Help that new team member understand the importance of his or her role within the big picture, by explaining, "Here's how your role fits in our overall mission and vision."

3. Discuss "How We Sell"

According to a recent Harvard Business School study, 71 percent of employees cannot explain their company's go-to-market strategy.[16] That's staggering, isn't it? Imagine the potential that communicating and reinforcing these ideas during new hire onboarding could unleash!

Teaching your newly hired team members about your company's go-to-market strategy is straightforward. Simply explain to your new employee about who your company's ideal customer is and what message is most attractive to them. Cover these questions:

- Who's your ideal customer?

- What industries are they in?

- How many employees do they have?

---

16   "When CEOs Talk Strategy, Is Anyone Listening?" Harvard Business Review, June 2003, https://hbr.org/2013/06/when-ceos-talk-strategy-is-anyone-listening/ar/1.

- What are their biggest challenges?
- Which one of these challenges do we solve for them?
- What's the competitive landscape?
- Who are our biggest competitors?
- When we win, why do we win?
- When we lose, why do we lose?
- Why do people buy from us?
- What do we do that's unique and differentiated?

4. Walk through Your Organizational Chart

The fourth step in the onboarding process is to walk your new employee through your company's organizational chart and discuss how they fit into it. Again, the goal is to help the employee understand how they can help the company achieve its vision and mission by feeling connected to the big picture regardless of what role they perform.

Although this step might seem like an obvious one when it comes to executive-level positions, it's just as important if the person is a front-line employee. These roles are the ones that *most* influence your customer's experience with the company. It's your challenge as a leader to inspire everyone and provide meaning for the role they are fulfilling. If you can't do that for everyone in your organization, you'll face real roadblocks in your ability to onboard and retain your best people.

It doesn't take a high level of effort to deliver a positive experience to new hires; it simply requires planning and a process. Many companies miss big opportunities to build a foundation for retaining top people by ignoring these simple details.

Consider what it will be like when your new hire gets home after their first day on the job. What do they tell their spouse or significant other about their day? Do they begin by complaining that they were forced to wait in the lobby for half an hour before anyone even acknowledged them? Or maybe their desk and computer weren't set up and they spent the bulk of the day stuffed in a conference room filling out reams of paperwork?

"They just didn't feel ready for me," your new employee might say. That's a not a great start to a new career, is it?

What if the experience your new employee shared at home was that someone greeted them at the door and walked them to their desk? What if they were given some balloons and a handwritten note describing how excited everyone is to have them on board? Or maybe they met every manager in the company and learned about how important their role is for the company to fulfill its mission, vision, and values?

"I can't believe what a great choice I made," your new employee might say. "This place is *awesome*."

Do you think that person is primed to have a long career with your organization? You bet.

Case Study: The Importance of Onboarding

Candice Crane of Crane Automotive, a human capital management consultancy, says that too many companies treat the onboarding process as simply the chance to cover legal and compliance issues. She believes this is a missed retention opportunity. She is a believer in the onboarding process as a way to indoctrinate new employees in the culture and direction of an organization as soon as possible.

"You need to teach them about what the company stands for, where it's going, and how you as an employee can get the most of your experience," she says.

Crane says that the best thing an employer can do for new employees in their first sixty days on the job is to help them understand what their role is and what is expected of them in terms of measureable performance.

"The quicker the company can define what they want, the quicker an employee can be influential," she says.

Another important tactic is to have the hiring manager check in with new employees twice a day—first thing in the morning and again at the end of the day—to help establish a consistent feedback loop that helps the employee understand how the company operates and how their role affects that performance.

Crane is also a proponent for career pathing, or helping employees understand what their next job might look like in the organization if they perform well. She began her career at Enterprise, which promoted people based on their performance rather than on seniority.

"If you want to retain your best employees, it's important to send the message to them that they are in control of their career," says Crane.

Evaluating Your Candidate's 30/60/90-Day Performance Plan

Earlier in chapter six, I discussed the concept of giving your final candidate a homework assignment—the 30/60/90-day performance plan. Now that we've onboarded your new employee, it's time to check in on how their performance is matching up with what you both outlined during your interview process.

The beauty of working through the performance plan during the interview is that you have an objective way to measure how your new employee is delivering on those expectations after they come on board. After their first thirty days on the job, you should sit down with them and evaluate whether they hit the outcomes they committed to hitting. Say, "Let's review the plan we developed together before you started."

- What do you feel is working?
- What do you feel isn't working?
- How are you feeling?
- Are you enjoying your new role?
- Have you accomplished the goals that we set together when you started?
- What can I be doing differently to help you achieve these goals?

The 30/60/90-day performance place is an extremely effective way to remove emotion from the conversation: either they succeeded at their plan or they didn't. This approach then allows you to make fast decisions about whether you made a mistake somewhere in the hiring process. It's not a matter of whether you like or don't like the employee; it's about whether they fit in your organization based on a set of objective outcomes.

If at thirty days they've missed their plan, it becomes decision time for you. Is there a coaching opportunity here, or was there something that prevented your employee from hitting their targets? Ditto for sixty days and ninety days. If someone is consistently missing their targets at this point, you'll find that, most of the time, they'll choose to opt out and quit all on their own.

Keeping Your Best People Motivated and Happy

As we noted earlier, when managers keep their promises, they retain their best people. Good people leave when they deliver on what they promised to do but the company fails to do the same.

When you reach that ninety-day milestone with your employees, it's time to confirm that everyone is still on the right path. It's a check-in. If you have done your job properly up front, you have set your new employee up to be happy in their role—including their compensation. There should be no surprises.

Does the employee still believe their role is helping the organization fulfill its mission? Do they like their job? How are they feeling about their performance? Do they have the skills and capabilities to succeed at their job? How about the organization—is it fulfilling its promises?

Conversations like this give you the opportunity to ask your new employees if they still see themselves as on the right path and, if not, how you as their manager might help them get back on it. It's also the chance for you to share your feelings about their performance.

This is such a valuable exercise, you should continue having these conversations every quarter moving forward.

．　．　．

CHAPTER SUMMARY

A new hire's first days on the job go a long way in deciding whether they stay with the job over the long term. Having a solid onboarding process is a crucial part of reducing turnover and boosting the retention rates of great employees.

A key part of the onboarding process should include making sure the new hire understands the mission, vision, and values of your business and how their role supports them. The new hire should also understand how their role fits in with others in the organization and how they might be able to grow their own career path.

You should also be using the 30/60/90-day performance plan you had your new hire complete during the interview process to measure their performance and ensure that candidate's expectations and the company's expectations are being met. The biggest cause of turnover in any organization is broken promises; use the first ninety days to make sure you are holding up your end of the bargain. If the new hire fails to perform, you must ask them to leave quickly. Be slow to hire but fast to fire.

SELF-ANALYSIS

Ask yourself the following questions:

- What onboarding process do you use?

- Do you have a script for what a new employee should expect in their first thirty to ninety days on the job?

- Have you ever broken a promise to a new hire? If so, what happened?

KEY TAKEAWAYS

1 Implement a robust onboarding process and you will have the best chance of retaining your top employees.

2 Make the time to explain how your new employees fit in your organization and how they will help meet its goals. This is essential to keeping them long term.

3 Be slow to hire but fast to fire if a new employee doesn't meet the expectations that you mutually set during the interview process.

ACKNOWLEDGMENTS

There are so many amazing individuals who contributed to this effort. Darren Dahl, my writing partner on this manuscript, made the case studies come alive and was instrumental in making sure the result was a great one. Christen Calloway, Hireology's Winston Wolf, kept me on track and focused, proofread and edited all the things, and managed the production schedule like the fate of the world depended on it. A big thank-you to Devin Law, whose illustrations so enhanced the quality of this book. To the crew at Greenleaf: thank you for believing in my vision for this book and helping bring it to reality.

The entrepreneurs and business leaders featured in this book gave their time, energy, and wisdom to this project and did so for no other reason than to be helpful and share their experience with the world. Thank you, all.

Most importantly, I want express my gratitude to my family, whose unwavering support makes everything I do possible.

And finally, a huge high five shout-out to the entire team at Hireology, who prove every day that the best team does, in fact, win. (Own it!)

INDEX

T

ABOUT THE AUTHOR

Adam Robinson is the cofounder and CEO of Hireology (www .Hireology.com), where he's on a mission to help business owners make better hiring decisions using predictive data and innovative technology. He is a noted recruiting industry expert, speaker, and author with over twenty years of experience in the field of hiring and selection management.

In 2016, Robinson was named to the Chicago Tech50 list of the city's top technology entrepreneurs by *Crain's Chicago Business*. Robinson was added to the *Chicago Tribune*'s Blue Network, a listing of Chicago's most influential entrepreneurs and innovators, and named a "Top 25 HR Industry Game Changer Under 40" in 2015 by *Workforce* magazine. Under his leadership, Hireology was named #94 on the 2016 Inc. 500 list, and has been recognized nationally by *Entrepreneur* magazine as a "Top Company Culture" and by *Crain's Chicago Business* as a "Best Places to Work" for both Millennials and Gen X. Hireology was named the "#1 Talent Management Platform" in 2014, 2015, and 2016 and "#1 in Customer Service" in 2013, 2014, 2015, and 2016 by *Human Resources Online* magazine.

Adam is passionate about entrepreneurship, donating time to a number of organizations that support the entrepreneurial cause. Through multiple leadership roles at Entrepreneurs' Organization (www.eonetwork.org), he has helped to develop and launch programs that teach core business skills to early-stage entrepreneurs around the world.

Adam has a BA from the University of Illinois at Urbana-Champaign, and received his MBA from DePaul University. He's a member of the Economic Club of Chicago.

Download interview guides, candidate scorecards, and other free tools at

www.thebestteamwins.com

Subscribe to The Best Team Wins Podcast:

Where leading entrepreneurs and executives talk about building their best team.